"I want to die with a flag"

by
Vartkes Nalbandian

I WANT TO DIE WITH A FLAG
ETHIOPIA: MY DELUSIONS AND DISILLUSIONMENT

Canadian Intellectual Property Office | An Agency of Industry Canada

I Want to Die With A Flag
Copyright Registration No.: 1156991 © February 14, 2019

© 2019 Vartkes Nalbandian

All Rights Reserved

No portion of this book may be reproduced in any form or by any means (which includes mechanically, electronically, or by any other means, including photocopying), without written permission from the author. Permission should be addressed in writing to vartkes@sassounent.com

Disclaimer
This book contains the ideas and opinions of its author. The intention of this book is to provide information, helpful content and motivation to readers about on the subjects addressed. It is shared and sold with the understanding that the author is not engaged to render any type of opinions, psychological, medical, legal or any other kind of personal or professional advice. The author has tried to recreate events, locales and conversations from memories of them. In order to maintain their anonymity in some instances, names of individuals and places may have been changed. Identifying characteristics and details such a physical properties, occupations and places of residence may have been changed as well. No warranties or guarantees are expressed or implied by the author's choice to include any of the content in this volume. The author shall not be liable for any physical, psychological, emotional, financial or commercial damages, including, but not limited to, special, incidental, consequential or other damages. The reader is responsible for their own choices, actions and results.

1st Edition, 1st printing 2019

Cover design by Carolyn Flower International - www.carolyflower.com
Interior design by Carolyn Flower International - www.carolyflower.com
Back Cover Author headshot by Taline Nalbandian
Interior Author photo by Taline Nalbandian

ISBN: 9781796675160
Imprint: Independently Published

DEDICATION

First and foremost, I dedicate this work to my beloved wife Mary Sakadjian Nalbandian without whose relentless support for the past forty years and beyond, I would not have succeeded in achieving all that I did in life.

I also dedicate this book to my younger sister Salpi, with whom we have a profound understanding and collaboration even in silence.

The completion of this book I owe it to my daughter Elise who is a source of constant encouragement and support for me.

My sons Garen and Raffi always have stood by me, but especially so during the last year which enabled me to achieve my dream of writing a book.

The support of my late elder sister Hermine and her husband Arakel helped me achieve many of the goals in managing the problems of the Armenian Community.

The support of my brother Harout and his wife Seza and their children, during the past year was very important for me to finish this book.

My dedication of this book goes posthumously to Avedis Terzian, Sahag Boghossian, Garbis Ebeyan and Moushegh Terzian for imparting their knowledge and experience, which I have used throughout the years.

My profound thanks go to the Addis Ababa University and the Embassy of Portugal in Ethiopia and particularly to the then ambassador His Excellency Antonio Cotrim and Dr. Isabella Boavida, who invited me to present the Ethiopian-Armenian history during the celebrations of the 500th anniversary of Ethiopian and Portuguese relations.

Similarly, I would like to thank the Tekeyan Cultural Centre of Montreal and the president of the association Berj Kokorian and Harout Nalbandian for organizing an Ethiopian-Armenian evening, where I presented our history.

The Haigazian University of Beirut for the past few years has been organizing events where the history of different diaspora centers is presented in a weeklong seminar. Upon the suggestion of Bishop Ashot Mnatsakanian, Dr. Antranik Dakessian included me to take part in that seminar, where I presented the history of Ethiopian-Armenians. I would like to thank both the University and the individuals who gave me this opportunity.

My appreciation and thanks for their contribution goes to, my mother Elise, my uncles Assadour and Dikran, friends Mgrdich Makhassian and his wife Shake, Francis Falcetto, Hampartzoum Ghazarossian, Boris Adjemian, George Israelian and Vahakn Karibian.

I want to thank also my niece Taline Nalbandian for my headshots for the book. And Kris Easter for proof-reading the book.

Finally, I wish to thank my friend Ketema Assefa for his support and friendship during the past thirty-five years.

Last but not least, I could not have done this project without Clint Ward who introduced me to Carolyn Flower. Without Carolyn and her team, Steve Walters and Shari Reinhart, this book would not have become a reality.

PREVIEW

I had the great honor and real pleasure to get to know Vartkes Nalbandian and his family in Addis Ababa. I say that without hesitation, because, even though I have lived across the world these past 30 years, I have rarely, if ever met, a man, and family, with such dedication to their family, culture and country, as Vartkes and the Nalbandians. And their nation is Ethiopia.

Ethiopia is a wonderful nation, rich in history and culture, and with a people intensely aware and proud of their identity. It is a nation that has welcomed people over the centuries, and today continues that tradition hosting large numbers of refugees displaced by conflict in neighboring countries.

Vartkes tells an intensely personal story of a family, and a community, displaced from their native land, Armenia, that found a home where they could build new lives, raise families, and become part of a rich and dynamic history. That was Ethiopia. The story traces events across a turbulent century of development, triumph, happiness, tragedy, chaos, and occasional despair, but a story that never loses hope, and retains throughout a powerful determination to survive, and succeed.

The story is powerful, sweeping, and deeply personal, and one cannot leave the book without a deep sense of connection to a man, and family, intensely loyal and committed to a nation, Ethiopia, and family. It is an inspiring and deeply moving read.

The book's cover is striking, like the book, showing a survivor of the atrocities committed by the Ottomans fled one homeland in Armenia and found refuge in Ethiopia, with the sole objective of creating a new homeland. The flag is Ethiopia's Imperial flag, which Vartkes chose because it is the flag of the Solomonic dynasty whose last three emperors, Yohannes IV (a start), Menelik (extensively), and Haile Selassie (profoundly), gave refuge to Armenians and enabled them to build new lives and create that homeland.

The books title captures the deep emotions of the author and his family, and their deep commitment to Ethiopia. "I want to Die with a Flag" tells the reader that the Nalbandians, ethnic Armenians in Ethiopia, wanted nothing more than to belong to a homeland, a desire captured so eloquently in the first page of the book which shows that what Armenians in Ethiopia wanted more than anything else was to gain Ethiopian citizenship.

Vartkes Nalbandian is a very special person, with a unique story to tell. Highly educated, brought up in a family with impressive artistic and intellectual talents, Vartkes is a third generation Ethiopian Armenian born in Ethiopia. The son of Nerses Nalbandian, considered by many the father of modern Ethiopian popular music, he is deeply rooted in Ethiopia with a profound understanding of Ethiopia's national mentality, traditions and customs. In this book, Vartkes has tried to capture those qualities when describing the sprawling, chaotic history he witnessed across the 20th century, and to share the views of a man deeply loyal to his nation and family, but caught up in the intense, complicated and overwhelming waves of history with the hope of offering future generations of Ethiopians an alternative, Ethiopian, perspective.

I came to know Vartkes through his wife, Mary. When I arrived with my family in Addis Ababa in 2014, we searched for a piano teacher for our son, and were introduced to a Mary Nalbandian, a woman of great warmth and elegance, who, for us, fortunately agreed to take our son, Colin, as a pupil. Over time, we met her children, Garen, Elise and Raffi, her sister-in-law Salpi, and her husband Vartkes. We enjoyed long and deeply personal conversations over delicious dinners during a period of intense political and social change in Ethiopia. I learned of their love for Ethiopia, their incredible musical talents, where it seemed each family member could sit at a piano at any moment and play the most beautiful music, and their integrity, passion for life, and profound belief in family and nation.

The book captures many of these qualities in intimate detail, and offers lessons to all of us about what is important in life. Vartkes shares his respect and love for his father and his family. His father, Nerses, was a powerful person in Ethiopian music history and the Ethiopian Armenian community. He describes in great detail his family's struggle to survive and succeed, with the single longest chapter recounting in fascinating detail his problematic experience with the Ethiopian leather industry. For me, perhaps one of the most powerful and symbolic stories is the one he tells of the Armenian school, the struggle to found, build and defend it, which culminated with the decision to transform the school and accept Ethiopian students, offering to the public a private school education for a very low fee, and which was a new contribution to Ethiopia..

Yes, the Nalbandians are part of an Armenian community, and proudly so. But they are Ethiopians as well, and the story Vartkes tells, of how they fought to preserve their culture and identity as Armenians in Ethiopia, is heroic. He tells the story of the power of education to a community, and how it can both unite and divide. In the end, the Armenian school was transformed, moving on from its pure Armenian origins, however difficult that may have been for the Vartkes and the community, and was re-opened as a new school for Ethiopians, and a testament to Vartkes' love and devotion to his homeland, Ethiopia

Vartkes recounts a story with unvarnished first-person truth. Yes, his English may not be perfect, and he may not tell his story in a straight line, but the story he tells is immensely powerful and deeply personal, and to me the imperfections capture some of the complexities and nuances of Ethiopia itself. I came to love Ethiopia, and to love the Nalbandians, and I am truly happy Vartkes has shared his impressions of Ethiopia's history over the last century. He offers a unique view that every reader can enjoy.

As he said himself,

"The observations and conversations within the pages of this book reflect my concerns, convictions and deep-rooted love for a country that I call home. It's true. I have very strong beliefs about the welfare of my beloved country, and I share all my inner thoughts with the public so struggles and survivals of Ethiopia can be seen and felt through my eyes. The eyes of a man who was there through this part of our history. I have the profound hope that by sharing the experiences of my family with Ethiopia it will open the hearts and minds of those in a position to help bring reform."

Enjoy the book, enjoy the honesty, and get to know a truly amazing person, family and nation.

David Kennedy

David Kennedy is a career member of the senior foreign service of the United States of America. He served in Ethiopia from 2014-2018

"I want to die with a flag"

A few months before she passed away, an elderly Armenian lady re-applied for the Ethiopian nationality and the officer in charge who saw she could barely walk, asked her:

- "Emamma," why do you want the citizenship?

And she replied:

- I want to die with a flag my son.

Orphaned in the deserts of Syria, near Deir-El-Zor, a survivor of the genocide, by a miracle and with the help of a nameless person, she found herself in an orphanage in Lebanon and was brought to Ethiopia as a bride. All her life she was stateless.

The pride and sense of belonging on her face when she got her citizenship was priceless.

For better or worse, she had her flag - the Ethiopian one - which is so heavily laden with meaning in Ethiopia and Africa.

Emamma is the Amharic word for a mother also used to address a senior woman.

CHAPTER ONE

It was December 14, 1960. Like every other Wednesday of the school year, we got up and got dressed, ate breakfast and headed out to school. And, like any other Wednesday, I'm sure we were being rushed so as not to be late, and I probably had some crucial homework assignment on my mind. What came next though, is something I remember vividly.

There was something about this day that felt different. There was tension in the air when we arrived at school. Our teachers were nervous; the director was busily on the phone having hushed conversations and was agitated. Students trying to get to school from the piazza had to return, deterred by tanks on the streets. Parents let their kids stay home, and some other parents rushed to the school, removing their kids from class, rushing back to their houses. My sisters, brother, cousins and I remained until the lunch break and then, once out of school we heard the repeating broadcasts about a coup-d'état that had occurred the previous evening. On December 13, 1960, Crown Prince Merid Azmach Asfa Wossen was pressured into broadcasting in favor of a new government, committed to "the progress of the country and its people." From the radios of neighboring houses and under the uncharacteristic silence of the playground, we heard the trembling voice of the Crown Prince, on the radio making this Wednesday unlike any other in my life, etched in the recesses of the mind, forever.

Back then we lived in Arat Kilo, and most of the students living nearby used to go home for lunch which is a 10 minutes' walk from what used to be the Armenian Kevorkoff School. Uncle Kegham in his Chevrolet van would pick us from the school at the regular time but contrary to his usual routine - instead of waiting for us parked in front of the Armenian Saint Kevork church – this time he was in the compound. He sent us back to our respective classrooms to collect all our books which we understood to mean we would not return to the school that day. Under any other circumstances, it would have been great fun to listen to our joyful uncle who could make the most mundane thing into an adventure, but on this day it was just scary, and he was pensive.

The ride back home to Arat Kilo was uncharacteristically silent, and I remember being all tensed up and shivering when we noticed a tank at the front gate of Berhanenea Selam Printing Press. The stillness of our typically hustling and bustling city was unsettling.

We arrived home to find my father and uncles gathered under the peach tree discussing the situation in town. We ate our lunches, hushed and hurried. I recall overhearing the elders exchanging thoughts over the military presence at all critical and relevant government offices. They were openly discussing their worries about the control of the imperial guard headed by the rebel leader Brigadier General Mengistu Neway.

The rumor was that other branches of the military, that were against participating in the coup, were advancing to reverse the action. That meant heavy clashes in the city, the stronghold of the Imperial Bodyguard. My mother and her sisters were flitting in and out picking up things and having whispered conversations with the men and generally hurrying us along. They cleaned the basement rooms and prepared some provisions. At about 2:30 PM the air force attacked Sidist Kilo. The electricity and the telephone lines were cut off, and fierce gunfire started.

Everyone from the Vorperian extended family was there except for Uncle Manuel and his family and our cousin Kevork who was at school. Uncle Assadour was in Italy on his honeymoon. I can recall Kevork's mother creating havoc on the street, threatening to go to Haile Selassie First secondary school near the Russian Embassy to find her son. My father had to physically pull her back into the compound when all reasoning failed. Sometime later with the sound of gunfire breaking the frightening silence in the background, Kevork cycled back from school had taken a two-hour trip which should have usually been a thirty-minute bicycle ride. It was an entertaining story - a real adventure. He had driven past military convoys and tanks and had to go under a bridge following a trail beside the Kebena River, and he wove a tale of his travels like a young Ulysses having braved monsters escaping, impossible odds. Sadly, the details of this exciting adventure elude me at the time.

Uncle Manuel also returned from his unsuccessful attempt to seek refuge as a British citizen in the British Embassy. That story I do not recall at all, but he was back.

The thing about our house in Arat Kilo is that it was always situated across some security building of the Government. Back then, the 2nd police station was across from our home, and many of the police with their families lived in the compound. One of them who had come to ask for water from our reserve advised us to barricade the gates for any eventuality. While we gave the policeman some water, that's when we found out that the water supply was cut too. In any case, we reinforced the doors and barricaded the gates, shut the aluminum and wooden shutters on all the windows in the house and fixed mattresses on the windows facing the front yard. We were expecting the worse and prepared for it as best we could. Sadly; we had to take the same precautions two more times in my lifetime.

These events that took place in late 1960 and early 1961 were a warning sign for the welfare of the Armenian Community in Ethiopia. Perhaps it was a sign for Ethiopia also that not all was well in the country like we used to believe. Looking back and talking to people who left Ethiopia in the 1960s and the 1970s, they remember Addis Ababa wistfully, describing it with nostalgia for its idyllic perfection. Having experienced the austerities that followed, my impressions are of course more nuanced and less rosy.

The first five-year plans after establishing the parliamentary reforms which were in effect since 1957 saw several changes such as the implementation of educational and social reforms. I may not have understood the complex issues of the coup, but I was reasonably sure that the demands of the coup organizers were like those proclaimed by parliament, making their claims meaningless.

Assessing the events now as an adult, I still hold that view and continue to think that a clear majority of the rebel's claims were opportunistic at worst or impatient at best. Based on the educational background of Brigadier General Mengistu Neway, one can deduce that the coup had a hidden agenda.

In 1945, the American Sinclair Oil Corporation entered the Ogaden region at the behest of Emperor Haile Selassie and in the late 1950s, there was general excitement about Sinclair finding vast reserves of oil in the Harerghe region in southern Ethiopia. An economic boom was expected but was hindered due to the citizens of Wardheer organizing mass demonstrations against them, surely instigated by foreigners.

The drilled holes were shut-off, and the oil exploration project disappeared. A few months later, new rumors emerged that Mr. Sinclair had appealed to Emperor Haile Selassie to go forward with the exploitation of the reserves. The stories died down eventually. The signboard, which was green with a yellow dinosaur of Sinclair Oil on the second bridge of Dukem disappeared a few years later as did talk of the findings. No one talked about oil. It was about this time that we had to learn a new name on the Ethiopian map, and this was the Ogaden.

The oil in Ogaden has always been a subject of controversy, even in the early 1900s when Sarkis Terzian had the monopoly of mining in the region some people brought him oil-bearing rocks, but others would bring news that the oil was introduced to the stones artificially. The question will always remain; why? The other issue that arises is if someone injected oil into the rocks, where did the oil come from? Regardless, the Armenians of Ethiopia had neither the resources to explore the oil nor did they have the possibility of finding the truth behind this anomaly.

These questions open the way to conspire with theories. Was the coup-d'etat connected with the Sinclair findings? My younger self would not have known to ask, but as I have grown older and seen so much more. I must wonder.

Meanwhile, there I was, a child amidst all this unrest and insecurity. Our mattresses were arranged on the floor in the middle room for the children as it had a window that opened towards the corridor between the two houses, it was the most secure room. Sleeping was difficult under the sound of the explosions and the thoughts that grew in my mind. War is not only what you learn about in history or watch unfold in movies. War lands at the doorstep of real people, in real time and it devastates families and communities.

We woke up on Thursday morning, to a shooting that continued to shatter the silence in the city center unabated from the previous afternoon. Despite that, the Armenian Baker Stepan distributed the bread, we still received our daily order.

The air raid continued but it seemed without bombing, we did not hear the deep tone of big bombs, which Uncle Dikran was imitating on his violin in his effort to entertain us. By early evening, the fierceness subsided, and some of the elders went out to assess the situation. Their first visit was to Sidist Kilo where the brothers of Uncle Kegham lived. Addis Ababa now had a deep crater at Sidist Kilo near the Martyr's monument and shattered glass in the piazza. Many also had a feeling of anxiety and malaise in a lot of people. At our house, we heard the news that amongst the persons summoned to the palace on the 13th of December was a person we knew Dejazmazh Letyibelew, the landlord of the house where the Aslanian brothers (Uncle Kegham's brothers) lived, and the family was distressed as there was no news about him.

The shooting continued the whole night through just as it did the previous night, but by Friday morning it had subsided significantly with only sporadic bullets being shot. Rumors circulated that Emperor Haile Selassie was on his way back to Ethiopia and with this news, the rebels hastily shot the 15 individuals summoned. Amongst them was the Dejazmach. This affected me profoundly as

I knew him to be a gentle and kind old man, who lived humbly in a small house having rented out the big one. Late in the afternoon, there was a commotion that the rebel leader had escaped towards the river behind our house and vanished thereof. General Mengistu Neway had fled, and troops were after him to bring him to justice.

Apparently, Emperor Haile Selassie had arrived at Asmara airport for a second triumphant entry into Addis Ababa, but unlike his previous entry on the 5th of May 1942, this one would be his demise.

On Monday, things began to settle and return to "normal" - well mostly anyway. Instead of the usual lessons, the subject at school was the sharing of personal experiences of the failed coup-d'état. Life continued as it always does and in my young, resilient mind, I believed that everything was all right again. Perhaps the only non-routine memories from that time and before are the memories linked to the coup-d'etat and its leader General Mengistu Neway and how he met his tragic end.

One afternoon I went to the music school with my father, which was somewhere near the St. Medhane Alem Church not far from the Embassy of the United States of America in Addis Ababa. We noticed that people were kissing the asphalt and others were following the elegant figure of Emperor Haile Selassie as he walked towards a building similar to the music school. After my father came back to the car, we learned that the Emperor was walking towards the court where the trial of General Mengistu Neway was in session. What a strange and eerie feeling to see the Emperor walking that day to the courthouse because on that same day, and at that same place Mengistu Neway was sentenced to hang. A few weeks later at the Menelik II Square behind the statue of Menelik II near The Saint Giorgis Cathedral, the population of Addis Ababa witnessed the rebel General's public hanging. The corpse of his brother Girmame, who had died in battle was hanged next to him.

Nothing was new for me. Even though only a child, I had already seen hanged persons twice before. It was hard to fathom, but it didn't scare me anymore. The first one definitely did scare me. It was near our school where someone had committed suicide, and it appeared that the person was still kicking. I ran away as fast as my legs could move. The second was near the gym where my older sister Hermine and I would go for our judo lessons twice a week; this was capital punishment for someone who had killed many innocent people.

The designated spot for the rebel hangings was in the clearings where the old structures had been removed for the upcoming construction of the modern complex of the municipality of Addis Ababa. It's interesting to note that public hangings are usually considered to be inhumane by the western media, and yet years, later the same press advertised and, in some cases, even celebrated the televised hanging of Saddam Hussein of Iraq.

CHAPTER TWO

Between 1955 and 1960 new Criminal and Civil Codes that would model European laws were being implemented in Ethiopia. The process of change was slow, mainly due to the reluctance on the part of the Ethiopian counterparts to accept the advice of Swiss experts who came to help, mostly because the changes would mean questioning the power of the Emperor.

Upon the interruption of the work, losing patience, the Swiss complained to Emperor Haile Selassie who in turn summoned his Ethiopian counterparts to find resolution and move the process along. After hearing their concerns regarding his governing power, Haile Selassie assured them they need not worry, "it is us that will implement and execute the laws." Changes accelerated considerably after the attempted coup-d'état, and by 1962 a working parliament was formed under Prime Minister Akliliu Habtewolde.

While this was an era of Ethiopianization, at the same time, it was a period that brought with it the alienation of the Armenians living in Ethiopia.

The educated elite Ethiopians amongst whom were women as well, acquired responsible positions thus opening an exciting chapter for Ethiopia, feminism, inclusion and other such modern concepts.

For Armenians, a question arose in those days "What is the future after Haile Selassie?" Within only a few months of the new codes, the few Armenians working in Ethiopian Airlines and the State Bank lost their jobs. A status of statelessness became the reality for of the Armenians, most of whom were already the second generation born in Ethiopia.

The Armenian presence in Ethiopia predates the Armenian Genocide. The first members of the present community started arriving in Ethiopia in 1871 and continued flocking in until the occupation of Ethiopia by Italy in 1936. Even the pioneers who came in 1871 were not the first. There was always an Armenian presence in Ethiopia since the forefathers of the two nations fought side-by-side in the year 1250BC during the Trojan war. An understanding and mutual trust was forged between these two nations even though there was no common boundary; they were ethnically different and from different continents. This continued up to the 20th century.

The centuries-old trust and understanding vanished, and the small hardworking Armenian community that did not exceed 1500 individuals at its peak started dwindling. The "stateless" status in ones country of birth was so offensive that it drove youngsters to conscript in the US army taking the risk of fighting in Vietnam. Emperor Haile Selassie denied citizenship to his allies who stood by him during the post-Menelik conflicts within Ethiopia. There were a few Armenians who remained favored by the Emperor, for example, the Yazedjian siblings Paylag and Anna, whose father Levon allegedly had produced a critical picture of Lidj Iyassu. Lidj Iyassu was the grandson of Emperor Menelik, the apparent heir to the throne. This picture was one of the reasons that shifted the popularity from Lidj Iyassu towards Ras Teferi Mekonen, who rose to power becoming the Regent of Ethiopia and finally crowned as Emperor Haile Selassie I. Even a few months before Professor Richard Pankhurst passed away, he used to ask me if I had come across evidence of that picture in the Armenian Community archives. I can honestly confirm that I have not, and it is not for the lack of looking for it.

The denial of citizenship continued, until the 1965 visit of the Catholicoses of the Armenian Church, Vazgen I of Etchmiadzin and Khoren I of the Holy See of Cilicia. Emperor Haile Selassie had invited them for a summit of the Eastern Orthodox churches. The Catholicoses had asked the Emperor to ease up the processing of citizenship for the Armenians born in Ethiopia. The request had some effect and the process eased up but did not become a birthright for the Armenians until the rule of the Derg. As an interesting aside, Emperor Haile Selassie succeeded to have the Coptic Orthodox Church of Alexandria, granting autocephaly (canonic independence for you and me) to the Ethiopian Orthodox Tewahedo Church in 1959. The Emperor extended an invitation to all the members of the Oriental Orthodox communion to a summit in Addis Ababa, which also asserted the position of Abune Basilios, the first Ethiopian Patriarch of the Ethiopian Church.

The systematic denial of citizenship touched every family.

In October 1961 Hermine, my older sister, attended the Armenian boarding school Melkonian in Cyprus. Our mother Elise accompanied her to settle Hermine in the boarding school. Hermine had a valid Ethiopian passport based on our father's citizenship. Our mother was traveling on an emergency travel document, a full A3 size paper folded in the middle with a photo on the front page. On her return, she visited Aleppo to meet the Nalbandians in Syria. The only memory she had of that excursion was the ordeal she faced at the border of Syria and Lebanon. Her travel document showed her Nationality as stateless even though she was a second generation born in Addis Ababa in 1927. Her mother who was also born in Ethiopia in 1905 was also "stateless."

Her application for citizenship was rejected several times, and the reason given was, she could not write Amharic. It seemed not to mean a thing to government that she could speak and read Amharic perfectly. The test was dictation from the Amharic daily newspaper Addis Zemen and though she handed over a paper written in Amharic after the tests she failed every time. The failing used to depress her. Until one evening after the test Tony Mavulian called and told our mother, not to be demoralized as Martha Gebretsadik, the person in charge of the citizenships in the Ministry of Foreign Affairs, without looking at the paper had thrown her test in the bin. Tony Mavulian had entered the room right after our mother for his routine Amharic proficiency test as well.

Why were a few Armenians in Ethiopia subjected to this citizenship test when it was common knowledge that nine out of ten inhabitants did not read or write back in those times? The Armenians who served Ethiopia diligently for many decades were subjected to this with little to no chance to pass the test.

The Armenian School had Amharic in its curriculum starting in the third grade since the unification of the two separate Armenian schools in 1934. With the Italian occupation of Ethiopia, our mother's generation was obliged to learn Italian as the Armenian School was taken over by the Fascist regime and converted into an Italian school named "Liceo Vittorio Emanuele II." The Italians canceled the Amharic classes altogether; an Armenian Catholic priest was brought from Italy, to teach the Armenian students the Armenian language and history. A year after the defeat of the Italians in 1942, Kevork Vorperian our maternal grandfather died, and our mother never continued her schooling.

Talking to people of their generation I found out that they started their education mostly at French schools, run by Jesuit priests and with the Italian invasion of 1936, everything changed to Italian and then to English. Most of that generation were fluent in these languages in addition to Amharic, Armenian and Turkish.

Armenians from the Middle East faced citizenship problems too, but in 1946, the French government started to distribute identification cards to Armenians and other nationals in Syria and Lebanon that were marked French Protectorate. That government gave a choice to take the local citizenships, and over half a million Armenians got Syrian or Lebanese citizenship, or they chose a French one. It was a limited time offer, and upon that limit, the holders of the identification automatically became Syrian or Lebanese. This decree by the French government applied to Armenians who were living in Ethiopia too. The information was kept a secret from many Armenians including my wife's father Paulos Sakadjian, who as a French subject had defended the French Embassy in Addis Ababa during the Italian occupation and was even wounded, but he was not aware of the announcement. Strangely enough, many Armenians born in Ethiopia, who had never been to Lebanon got Lebanese citizenship based on the French protectorate identification card.

CHAPTER THREE

After graduating from the Armenian Kevorkoff School of Addis Ababa in 1962, (our father believed in giving his children an Armenian-based education), it was my time to attend the Melkonian Educational Institute in Nicosia, Cyprus. I was initially turned away by the Ministry of Foreign Affairs when I asked for a passport. Finally, I was sent to the Ministry of Education to clarify if I merited the award of pursuing my education abroad. There I faced the attractive, but severe and bitter Sofia, who oversaw scholarships. The elegant lady with her long and perfectly manicured nails failed to understand that the opportunity to study at Melkonian was one that no one else from Ethiopia could benefit from.

For one thing, Melkonian was an Armenian boarding school that taught every subject in Armenian except English, French, and Greek or Arabic. Imagine that the fate of my secondary education was deliberated by a panel of people who knew nothing about me. These people got to decide whether they would allow me to study at a school for which I have a letter of acceptance, and they knew nothing about. "TheCommittee" decided that 500.00 Ethiopian Dollars would have to be deposited in my name to cover the cost of the scholarship and my return ticket. An illogical and incomprehensible decision, as the school, when giving me the opportunity to study there had not requested a guarantee against any payments or a return ticket. Besides, my father was on the payroll of the Ministry of Education, as a music teacher in the music school.

I could see nothing just or fair about it. Think about it: The Ethiopian government wasn't paying for my secondary education or the air tickets to go to the school and back. It was the unfortunate birth in Ethiopia of and the inherent behavior of incapable and indecisive government officials, which would continue to complicate life for many of us up to now.. They were avoiding an answer by hiding behind useless committee meetings. Twelve years later I claimed and got the deposit back. But that is another story of the astounding bureaucracy of which I have thousands.

Despite the illogical nationalism and frustrating discrimination, I did eventually get my passport and made my way to Cyprus. The Ethiopian Airlines Douglas DC6B aircraft took off from the old airport, and in June the next year, we landed in a Boeing 707, at Bole International airport for the first time. The single road connecting the airport to the stadium area was the only road to town. From the airport to the stadium was empty land up to the crossroad where the Investment Office now stands.

Each year, upon my return I was astonished to witness the developments of the roads, the modern villas built in Bole and the branching streets towards the villas. Addis Ababa was booming. The land being sold for development helped the economy with the circulation of money, but the gap between the wealthy and the poor was widening. One of the pioneers to venture into the Bole was Yeghia Chorbadjian, who built one of the first villas in Bole.

My father believed in planning for the future. One way that he enjoyed doing so was to invest in property as it would serve as security for old age, especially in a country where there are no plans or pensions for the elderly, except for government employees. He bought three plots of 1000 square meters each in Bole. My parents discussed building their dream home on one of them and the Swiss architect Mr. Pere came over to discuss the plans. We had our input on the project, but it was mainly our mother who gave the most, based on the impracticalities she had experienced as a housewife on our Arat Kilo house. The land was available in those days at a reasonable price.

I graduated from Melkonian in June 1967 and was supposed to leave Cyprus on the 7th of June to Addis Ababa, but all airlines had

"I Want to Die with a Flag"

canceled the flights, due to the war that broke out between Egypt and Israel. Instead of waiting in the school (as graduates the school did not welcome us anymore) three of my friends and I made a complete tour of Cyprus. Upon our return from the trip, we vacated the dormitory of the school. I had to go to a hotel for the last five days in Nicosia. My younger sister Salpi, who was also attending Melkonian had remained in Nicosia with friends. She had been selected by the school to spend the holidays in a summer camp in Armenia. We had such a great time together in Cyprus during my last few days.

The six-day war in the Middle East was over, and the airlines started picking up flights again. My friend John and I were booked on a flight to Cairo. When the plane landed, the devastation from the bombardment of the Cairo airport a few days earlier was apparent. In the space of less than a decade, I was once again faced with a city scarred by the violence of war. For the first time as a young adult, I understood the fear of how fragile life is and how a world event could impact just about any innocent bystander who has no stake in the issue. Through the blackened windows of the terminal, when I saw the Ethiopian Flag, on the tail of the aircraft that had landed at the Cairo airport at about 2:00 a.m. I sighed a breath of relief - I was going home for good.

All my fears vanished utterly half an hour after take-off and my nerves dissolved into joy, as I watched our descent begin into Asmara, a mere hour away from home while enjoying a delicious inflight breakfast.

Upon my return home, my priority was to apply to The Haile Selassie I University. I had my boarding school experience where I also learned to manage my own life but missed the family life and the outings to Assab, Arba Minch, and Awash. I wanted to stay at home in Ethiopia to enjoy family life. Unlike my older sister, who attended the University, with almost the same educational background as mine, I was rejected. I had no choice but to take a sabbatical. I decided to work on my citizenship and driver's license.

The driver's license was straightforward as I already had two years of driving experience. I had driven in Addis Ababa when the traffic was still on the left side, as introduced by the British in 1942. For about six months I did the inventory in Hagbes helping my aunt, but in January 1968, when I finished the work assigned to me, I quit and started helping my father with the piano tunings, repairs and the finishing of the Bole house, after the contractor had disappeared having taken excess advance money.

We worked on the finishing of the house, and when "Total" the French oil company rented it out before it was completed, we were forced to accelerate the final touches. It was an enjoyable experience for me to work closely with my mother on the completion of the construction, helping with the design and decorating of the gardens and the compound, based on the vast experience we had from our Bishoftu retreat.

Citizenship proved to be more difficult as the replacement of Martha Gebretsadik, Kebede Gebrewold had similar work ethics like his predecessor, but the vice-minister Merid Mengesha proved to be different.

We had met Merid Mengesha socially at a wedding. Two weeks later he saw me standing across his office in front of the door of his deputy, Mr. Kebede Gebrewold. As he entered his office, he greeted me. This came as a surprise since men of his position, especially in Ethiopia, would not usually acknowledge an acquaintance in the workplace, much less a teenager he just happened to share a table with at a wedding. After considerable time, he saw me again and asked what the problem was; I explained my situation also mentioned the citizenship applications of my aunt and my grandmother, whose files were together with mine, for reasons I do not know. He ordered the documents to be brought to him, and after examining them, he signed the ready citizenship cards and told me to collect the stamped citizenship papers from the archives. I rushed to pick up my aunt Marine from her house and went home to pick up my grandmother, and the three of us went to the Ministry of Foreign Affairs and got our citizenship cards. After many months of waiting, I obtained my citizenship not because he knew me, but because he had the proper work ethics. I often remember the instance of my encounter with this gentle person.

At that time, I looked at our family dossier and realized that the application for our father's citizenship had been repeatedly rejected based on a report that he is seeking the Ethiopian nationality to buy land. It enraged me that someone who taught music to hundreds of Ethiopians, someone whom they could not replace could have such strike against him. This report was later reversed due to his invaluable contributions and unmatched dedication to the development of Ethiopian music, but the report filed against my father was no small thing. It reminded me of one of the many stories our elders used to tell about Emperor Menelik II. Someone with an envious vendetta against Armenians had reported about an Armenian acquiring land and building a house on it to Emperor Menelik II. The Emperor replied, "let him build; he cannot take it with him to his country." How true it was after seventy years, the Derg expropriated the houses of many Armenians as "extra houses".

All my documents were up-to-date as I waited for the reply to my reapplication from the University. To my dismay, I got another refusal. As a result, I accepted the scholarship which had come in my name from the Armenian Soviet Socialist Republic and prepared myself to go there. No longer upset about the repeated rejections to attend the school of my choice, I began to look forward to this new chapter in my life, especially since I found out that girlfriend from Melkonian was planning on attending university in Yerevan as well. Little did I know at the time that this would soon carry with it, disappointment and heartbreak.

At the time of my leaving, USSR invaded Prague, and sure enough, this affected the issuance of my visa. I did not understand how my entry into the USSR would be affecting the invasion, but the Soviet Embassy in Addis Ababa managed to delay my visa, characteristic of how people in government make some ludicrous decisions.

I have many things to tell about the days of my education. My experience as a student at Melkonian and the University in Yerevan may be the subject of another book, in this one, I will stick to my memoirs in my country, Ethiopia.

CHAPTER FOUR

The businesses and lifestyle of the Armenians in Ethiopia had been developing over time and stabilized by the late fifties. Life had settled into a fine routine of work, leisure and family time. Weekend outings became the social highlight of every family. The trendy places to go were Bishoftu, Modjo, and Sebeta, and for the more adventurous ones, Sombeway and Ararobi were also popular - part of the rift valley lakes. The Ethiopian Rift Valley Lake region is a beautiful area with many alkaline lakes and gorgeous mountain ranges looming on the horizon. The lake formed by the Koka dam on the river Awash engulfed Sombeway and Ararobi Rift Valley lakes.

Lakes Shalla and Langano were trendy outings, mostly reserved for the longer holidays during Meskel, Ethiopian New Year and Timket. The two-hundred-kilometer drive on the gravel road through the acacia forests was lengthy and required preparations. But the great gatherings on the shore of these lakes started at that era and continue in Langano up to the present and the memories of those times still warm my heart today.

My recollection of our visit to Sombeway and Ararobi relates to the adventure we had one time when the back of our Ford pickup sank into quicksand. It took hours to bring the car out of it — the careful planning of my father and patient execution saved the vehicle with minor damages on the bumper. The lunch was a pre-prepared sandwich followed by the main course of fish from the lakes. As a young boy, I was not very keen on fish, but the whole outing was about the ponds and the big tilapia, which benefitted from all the nutrients that the Awash river brought from flooding during the rainy season. The river was pristine back then.

In Bishoftu, the Grand Hotel overlooked the Hora lake, ran by Paylag Yazedjian and this was the place to be for the weekend. The food was excellent, and its relatively glamorous casino hustled with people. I must say the hotel had not lost its charm even under the Ras Hotel management until its tragic end by the administration of the Midroc group, who, ignorant of the historical past of the hotel, preferred to blow up the site instead of using its historic charm.

In my opinion, Modjo had no appeal except for the fantastic entertainer, and host, Varoujan Antranigian. His simple menu and the whole lamb barbecued in the open air over their outdoor pit on Sundays kept card players flocking in for food and games over weekends throughout the entire year. In Sebeta twenty-five kilometers west, there was a restaurant just at the entrance of the village, which was run by Yeprem Keshishian and his family. I still remember the rabbits, chickens and pigs in the compound. It was a short outing for churchgoers, who also bought their vegetables on their way back to Addis Ababa.

Some members of the community, who were not churchgoers or card players chose to build houses in Bishoftu, either on Lake Cheleqlaqa or Bishoftu. Our mother's uncle Elias and our aunt Mary had their weekend houses, overlooking Lake Bishoftu. Ethnic Ethiopians avoided this lake as it was considered a place where the devil dwelled. One Sunday, at a party at Uncle Elias' house, our father left the compound heading towards the top of the hill. The next Sunday, we went again, parking the car and walking towards the top of the mountain that was adjacent to Uncle Elias' property, where we met the owner of the land. An agreement was made between my father and Woizero Atsede (Woizero is the Amharic word for Mrs.). During the next week, the paperwork was finalized, and the cornerstones fixed, and we started to build. Within a few weeks, a barbed wire fence and a wooded gate, marked our territory in Bishoftu. An orchard was planted, with mango, lemon, and lime, orange, pomegranate, plantain, papaya, mulberry trees. It scented the air with sweetness as the tree grew. Water delivered by donkey loads was used for the irrigation of the plants. An access road was imminent, but no one would agree to have a piece of their land cut for developing an access road even though it would serve them as well. My father purchased the land for the road from several inhabitants, who allegedly owned the plots. The property expanded and each time we dealt with another owner, who sold land to investing in agriculture.

Our father needed time off from his hectic schedule teaching music to the Haile Selassie I Theatre Orchestras, at Nazareth School, the Armenian School, the Theological College and the Music School. In addition to which he was also teaching and conducting the Armenian choir and the choir of the Haile Selassie University Glee club. He also tuned almost all the pianos in Addis Ababa and on Sundays he was in church for conducting the choir for the Holy Mass. Bishoftu was his relaxation. Once we converted the small hut into a habitable dwelling and installed electricity, we drove to Bishoftu every Saturday afternoon where our parents were engaged in gardening and my sisters and brother either helping them or swimming. The Ethiopian Air Force nearby had a cinema hall, and from time to time we would watch films there. Then, Sunday morning it was back to Addis, for church and back to Bishoftu after the Holy Mass. When there was no congestion on the road, it was a forty-five-minute drive at most to and from Addis.

The trip would take longer on Saturday afternoons as that is when Emperor Haile Selassie and his motorcade would be heading to the palace situated on grounds next to the Grand Hotel on Lake Hora. His convoy moved at a languid pace; therefore, the escorting motorcycles every so often gave priority to the other vehicles to pass the Emperor's limousine. The escorting group consisted of two bikes and a car behind the official vehicle. It amazes me that the escorting police allowed us to pass the Emperor; this would not ever happen again after the fall of the Emperor where roads are blocked for the Prime Minister and the President, to move in a long motorcade, starting some thirty minutes before the arrival of the procession.

His Imperial Majesty Haile Selassie the First, Elect of God, King of Kings of Ethiopia, was a man of the people and it was his habit to stop and talk to people. In transit to Bishoftu, he'd periodically stop, talking to people, shaking their hands and accepting petitions. It has been said that he even gave bread to the poor although this we never witnessed. This was not the situation with the "elected by the people" successors of the Emperor. On the contrary, instead of approaching they avoided contact with their electors. They took to the roads full speed ahead in motorcades of not less than twelve bulletproof cars and six motorbikes blocking roads, causing disruption and inconvenience with no regard for the people they were "elected" to serve. This is one small example of their interest in "freeing the people from the tyrannical imperialistic rule."

Our Bishoftu took us away from all of the city noise. We retreated to Bishoftu to unwind, relax and take our minds off daily hassles and troubles. It was an outing for our relatives and other family friends as well. We were joined by dear ones like the Chorbadjians, Garabed Poladian, an Armenian writer, who came to Ethiopia as the director of the Armenian School. The Lion Club, the Haile Selassie Theatre Orchestra and the Armenian choir also gathered there on more than one occasion. In group outing. And, Bishoftu was where our father did a lot of his creative work, especially the choral arrangements of Ethiopian songs for The Glee Club choir of the University supported by the girls of Nazareth School, which developed into a dynamic choir performing very popular concerts. Unfortunately, the success and fame were short-lived because the university had become heavily politicized against which the government retaliated with restrictions, and one of the first was the prohibition of social gatherings. The Glee club was closed and the choir dispersed.

Little groups of students and a few professors broke out with anti-government sentiments. Students became radically anti-government — a government that fed, clothed and gave a stipend as pocket money to each. The government and subsequently the country broke up. A professor of Geography in the class was preaching a philosophy of disobedience by saying: "if there is a poisoned glass and cleaning it proves to be difficult it is better to break it." The more the educated elite pushed, the more vigilant the government became, and the unrest led to the freedom of speech being suppressed, and the arts being heavily censored. The censorship ran to the extent that two favorite love songs of the time, (Amharic poetry usually contains a lot of double-entendres) arranged by our father for choir, "Eyeye" and "Ououta" were banned.

Despite all the political undercurrents at the time, Emperor Haile Selassie, ignoring the internal dissatisfaction, continued advocating uniting Africa, and thus in 1963, the Organization of the African Unity was formed. Regrettably, on the 50th anniversary of African Unity, Emperor Haile Selassie's name was barely mentioned, and he did not have a statue in the compound, amongst others who got the honor. He was someone who had sacrificed so much to bring the free African countries together and to support the rebels. For me, it was more than a shocking oversight; it was a blatant insult to the dedicated work of The Emperor. This omission brought back to memory President Keneth Kaunda of Zambia's speech in the 1980s, advocating for the "great leader of Ethiopia,", Mengistu Hailemariam. That speech of Kaunda disgusted me as he was one who had reaped the benefits of Emperor Haile Selassie as a freedom fighter. But politics is a dirty game. "The King is dead. Long live the King."

The opening ceremony of the OAU (Organization of African Unity) had to show the grandeur of Ethiopia, its leadership and black power, and it did. The reception of the delegates was impeccable, and the programs very well-rehearsed. Our father, Nerses Nalbandian was commissioned to compose an anthem for the opening as the musical director of the Haile Selassie Theatre. Disappointingly, on the 50th anniversary, this anthem was replaced by an inferior substitute. The Armenian Choir performed the "Africa" for the first time. The newspapers failed to find a subject for criticism, so they attacked the Amharic accent of the Armenians. It was a pathetic ploy by the journalists. For the official opening, our Father trained a choir of ethnic Ethiopians as required, but only two days before the performance he was told to stand behind the curtain and teach someone to mimic his moves. Our father understood the reason for this racial discrimination and humbly accepted the decision. Some of his students, infuriated by what had happened on that day objected. Merawi, a noted musician, still to this day remarks about that wrongdoing.

We are Ethiopians, and yet we are not.

CHAPTER FIVE

It was ironic that the author of the National Anthem of Ethiopia, "Ethiopia Hoy," Kevork Nalbandian passed away a few days before the formation of the Organization of African Unity. Was the timing of his death a warning to his nephew, Nerses Nalbandian?

Many articles and radio broadcasts regularly praise the work of our father, Nerses, and there are still some of his students who mention him and his work. However, unlike Nerses, there is no documentation and any mention of the contributions that his Uncle Kevork Nalbandian made. Besides being the author of several anthems, Kevork was also a teacher, composer, conductor; he trained Ethiopians to play music on European instruments. He was a prominent musician, a captain in the Imperial Bodyguard, the originator of the fanfare and the orchestra of the Imperial Bodyguard, and the organizer of the Hager Fikir Theatre, who had staged many musicals for the first time in Amharic.

And yet, when he died, Kevork was forgotten and neglected, laid to rest unceremoniously, with an insignificant funeral that lacked any show of appreciation for his contribution to the arts in Ethiopia. The entirety of his life and work went by without a trace and even more so when his only son, Jirayr, was married to an Italian lady, left Ethiopia for Italy after losing his position in the National Bank of Ethiopia.

There was no expression of gratitude to people who represented Ethiopia as an advanced nation during the coronation of Emperor Haile Selassie. When I think about the unceremonious entombment of Kevork Nalbandian, I'm triggered by the memory of many other Armenians whose work is also unrecognized, unheralded by Ethiopians and who rest in that cemetery as well, both before and after Kevork Nalbandian.

Boghos Markarian

In Zuquala rests the pioneer of the present Armenian Community, Boghos Markarian. Boghos had earned the trust of two emperors and served as an envoy between Emperor Yohannes IV and Ras Sahlemariam Haile Melekot (Emperor Menelik II). When he was sent to Lome by Ras Sahlemariam to the court of Dejazmach Girmame to collect the taxes, he had collected more than anyone else in the years before him, and this won him the confidence of Ras Sahlemariam. Ras Sahlemariam was so pleased with the higher amount of tax money collected over previous years that he appointed Markarian as an advisor and included him in delegations and as an envoy. Markarian accompanied Ras Berru to the court of Ismail Pasha in Egypt. It was during this trip that the treaty that paved the way for Ras Sahlemariam to assume the throne of Ethiopia was signed. Boghos Markarian's role in this and many other such commendable expeditions was never mentioned. Boghos Markarian served Ethiopia with devotion, and this devotion deserves at least a mention, but none was ever made. Why was it necessary for Emperor Menelik II to include him in the delegation?

Dikran Ebeyan

In the Armenian cemetery rests Dikran Ebeyan. Dikran was the man who made the crowns that are exhibited in the Entoto Mariam museum. Besides the crowns made by Dikran Ebeyan, there is the one presented to Emperor Menelik II by the Italian government. Emperor Menelik refused to wear it as can be seen by the perfect untarnished condition it is in. He felt that by wearing the crown, he'd become a subject of the Italians. The guide in the museum has no idea about the coronets and no clue of the significance of what is displayed there. It should be the duty of the historians to educate the curators on the history, the significance and details of each object, instead of rewriting history with every change of government. And it is the duty of historians to cover all aspects of the past they study and write about, for an unbiased picture of the whole story. The work of Dikran Ebeyan, which had preference over the finely made Italian crown by Emperor Menelik II is worthy of mention.

Levon Yazedjian

The anecdotes connected with the murals of Gibi Gabriel and Entoto Mariam concerning Emperor Menelik and Itegue Taytu, both by Levon Yazedjian are exciting stories that visitors will enjoy hearing while visiting these churches. Emperor Menelik gave Levon plots in Addis Ababa against payment for his work, Emperor Menelik also diplomatically intervened with Sultan Abdul Hamid of the Ottoman Empire for the release of Levon's family, and there will be evidence of these in the archives that reveal the truth. The name Levon Yazedjian is unknown to the present and will remain unknown to generations that come.

Krikor Hovian

Has anyone today heard the name of Academician Krikor Hovian? Likely not. He built the first twelve bridges of Addis Ababa. The one near the German Embassy still being used today is more than a century old. The other bridges did not collapse but had to yield to modernization and development. Krikor Hovian who built the Taytu Hotel and the bullet factory also established and headed the engineering department of the Municipality of Addis Ababa. His work is worthy of recognition, and the history books and records of Addis Ababa should at least bear mention of him.

Minas Kherbekian

Minas Kherbekian was a student of Krikor Hovian, and he eventually took over the civil engineering work of Addis Ababa from

Hovian. He is negatively renowned as "Minas the demolisher." As the civil engineer of Addis Ababa, he is known as the one who demolished illegally built houses, alas there is no mention of all his other work. He also made Entoto Mariam, Ourael, Teklehaimanot, Mitake Emanuel, Entoto Kidanemihret and many other churches. As well, he constructed the bell tower of Giorgis and the mausoleums in Selassie, Stephanos, and Entoto Mariam. He paved over two hundred kilometers of roads within Addis Ababa and thousands of kilometers of trails in the rest of Ethiopia. Instead of the antagonistic perception of him as the demolisher that history wrote, he should be recognized as an exemplary government employee who was responsible for building up churches, towers, and mausoleums; as one who devoted his life to the development of Ethiopia.

Sarkis Terzian

Sarkis Terzian, the man who brought the first steam engine to Addis Ababa from England in 1905, is depicted as the man with the broken engine. Besides paving, flattening and grinding stones, it also had an attachment to mill grain for food. The epigrams about "Sarkis Babour" or "Sebara Babour" meaning broken engine, do not do justice to Sarkis Terzian. The steam engine stood idle after the assassination of its owner Sarkis Terzian. I've seen it myself, erected near the Ministry of Information and its remnants were removed during the construction of the new complex of the Municipality of Addis Ababa.

Instead of depicting the idleness of the Fowler, the bravery and sacrifice Sarkis Terzian has done for Ethiopia are worth mentioning. Emperor Menelik II knew the limitations of sending an ethnic Ethiopian to Europe to bring arms, so he entrusted Sarkis Terzian instead with significant funds, gold, and ivory, to buy weapons and ammunition before the battle of Adua. Sarkis fulfilled this duty and smuggled canons, guns, and ammo into Ethiopia under the watchful eyes of the Italians. Having no family at the time, he could have easily chosen to defect, but his loyalty to Ethiopia and Emperor Menelik II prevailed. His heroism should be marked and noted in the history of Ethiopia regardless of ethnicity, as an example for future generations of Ethiopians.

Hagop Baghdassarian

Professor Wolfgang Hahn of the University of Vienna mentions the work of Hagop Baghdassarian in his research of Ethiopian coinage. When the Emperor asked his statesmen what, in the unification of Ethiopia was still missing, it was Baghdassarian who suggested minting coins, thus initiating and producing the minting of the Menelik coins with the help of Michael Topdjian. At the time, Ethiopia was still using Austrian Maria Theresa silver coins as currency. In his lifetime, Baghdassarian, who was invited to Ethiopia by Ras Mekonen, served Emperor Menelik II, Itegue Taytu, Lij Iyassu, Empress Zewditu, and Emperor Haile Selassie and yet for all his contributions, his heirs did not even inherit his own house. Does this show appreciation for his contribution to the country?

The Boyadjian Family

Thankfully, due to the announcements of the Embassy of France in Ethiopia and the work of Professor Berhanu Abebe, the work of the Boyadjian Family as the official photographers of the Imperial Court of Ethiopia was celebrated. A visual exhibition portrayed the history of the country through their photography. The irony is, the exhibition was organized by the "Jeu de Pomme" museum of Paris and displayed there so still, in Ethiopia their work went by unrecognized. It is overwhelming the realization that Emperors trusted the family and stood in front of the camera, without fear of assassination.

Skunder Boghossian

Even though Alexander (Skunder) Boghossian the Ethiopian abstract artist, has an Armenian name, his work was appreciated and the school of arts of the Addis Ababa University bears his name. This acknowledgment he owes it not only for his incredible talent, his numerous works but also for his genetic makeup.

There are many Armenians who have contributed to Ethiopia with their skill, knowledge, and innovations but to name them all might be the subject of another book. As far as my own personal recollections go, there was seldom an Armenian recognized for their excellence in citizenship.

CHAPTER SIX

Whenever there was a school holiday, I would return home, excited about spending time with my family. It was always interesting, with every trip home to see the progress and the changes in Addis Ababa, and of the Armenian Community. There was exponential growth in every area.

Both the government with Agricultural Development Units in Southern Ethiopia and investors most of whom were Ethiopian landowners and educated Ethiopians preferred to be in agriculture rather than working in offices. New foreign investors and the old international communities were investing heavily in commercial agriculture, share holder companies emerged. Shares began to be traded in an office across from the Ministry of Education, and many Armenians were investing in stocks. A few Armenians also ventured into modern farming and agriculture at a small scale.

Ethiopia was exporting haricot beans to Europe in direct competition with the United States of America. Unknown words like haricot beans had become a day-to-day subject of discussion. By 1972 the agricultural exports of Ethiopia had reached a quarter of a percent of the overall world agricultural trade. An impressive figure, the effect of which amazed me every time I went home for vacation. The country was enjoying a favorable balance of trade and had a gold reserve against its currency. Ethiopia did not need loans from the IMF or the World Bank.

Events that followed and the belief of many developing countries made me wonder, "Would a developing country be allowed to be self sufficient?" From what I have witnessed so far, the answer is, no.

Industrial development was visible too. After the completion of the Koka dam in 1960, the Italians got full amnesty and started investing in Addis Ababa. Many Italians from Asmara began opening branches in Addis Ababa in the construction, import-export, manufacturing and trading sectors. Addis Ababa was booming. Emancipated new blood came to Addis Ababa, changing the pace of the growth and the complexion of the city.

One building after another mushroomed up. Italian and French architects opened offices in Addis Ababa, and you could read the names on the boards of each construction site. Mezzedimi realized the ECA complex, the Addis Ababa City Hall, ERESCO building and the Armenian Community building. The Commercial and National Bank of Ethiopia across from the Ministry of Defense was a design of Henry Chomet and built by Varnero. Various structures created in those years are landmarks in Addis Ababa, like the Berhanena Selam Printing Press, The Hilton Addis Ababa, the General Post Office, The Ministry of Foreign Affairs, The Saint Paul Hospital, The Duke of Harar Memorial Hospital (Black Lion) and many others. The wide roads that complemented these structures were opened giving Addis Ababa a majestic look. There was no mistaking that Addis Ababa was booming from a busy village life into a city thriving with growth.

The construction boom boosted local production of building material, replacing imported items and with material of good quality; like chipped wood boards, soft boards, acoustic ceiling tiles, high-quality doors, door and window frames, the concrete reinforcing bars and marble and cement tiles. The furniture industry was expanding, locally manufactured goods surpassed the quality of items imported to Ethiopia before this.

Italians, Greeks, and Armenians who were heavily involved in industries continued expanding their production until 1975. The textile and ginning, leather and shoe, printing and paper converting, flour milling, wood and furniture industries were undergoing significant expansion and modernization. Ethiopia was in profound development, not only statistically but also visually. Growth was tangible.

Culturally, there was also development in Ethiopia in general and within the Armenian Community. During my absence from Ethiopia, the Armenian Community cultural activities expanded. Already by the late 1950s, there were two string quartets and the Mouradian choir. In the 1960s apart from the Mouradian choir, there was a quartet by the Djerrahian family, with Aida Bassmadjian at the piano occasionally. There were performances of Armenian satirical dramas regularly, sometimes with known Armenian artists from the Middle East performing. At the beginning of the 1970s, a dance and choir ensemble delivered a much talked about performance under the leadership of my uncle, Dikran Vorperian, a professional lyric tenor and violinist. Dikran also gave solo concerts bringing classical opera singing into Addis Ababa.

Pre-revolution Addis Ababa was very promising in all aspects; construction, agriculture, industrialization, commerce, culture, and entertainment. Despite that, the exodus of Armenians increased at an alarming pace. It saddened me greatly. There was a general feeling of betrayal, even abandonment. I could not talk to my uncles who were preparing to leave for Australia, wondering, where was their commitment to our family members who started to emigrate to build a new life. It disturbed me that with all this growth and transformation, people who had come to Addis Ababa with nothing TO nothing, when there were not even proper houses, were just leaving everything they built and achieved behind. Families who had endured life in huts with no electricity and water supply, before the Italian occupation were abandoning a comfortable life that through hard work, their predecessors had secured. The astonishing fact was, all those who were emigrating were from the Piazza area or had close contact with the local population. It was a riddle I wanted to solve.

For the most part, Armenians were unaware of the political undercurrents in Ethiopia. After the assassination of Hovhannes Semerdjibashian, who allegedly pledged allegiance to Ras Hailu of Gojam to revolt against Emperor Haile Selassie, there were no Armenians left working in the palace or for the government whereas in the early 1900s many Armenians were employed by the government.

There was a lot of unrest under all the pomp and glamour in Addis Ababa. The poor were getting poorer as the cost of living rose and the middle class, feeling the economic strain, grew uneasy, impatient and more demanding. It was a common occurrence for the street boys to verbally abuse and blame the "ferenjis" (Greeks and Armenians) for all the problems in the country.

My grandmother used to tell a story about Emperor Menelik. She recounted how he had scouts who were sent out to the market to eavesdrop on what people were talking about and then report to back to the sovereign. Once, when the scouts came back with no news, Menelik told them to spread false rumors to keep the people otherwise occupied. Were the verbal assaults on the "Ferenjus" is a consequence of such rumors?

The students and the university, in general, were otherwise occupied busy organizing a foundation for the dismantling of Ethiopia.

The Eritreans constituted a significant percentage in the university compared to their overall numbers' vis-a-vis the total population of Ethiopia, and they enjoyed many privileges. A lot of them had important positions both in the army and in government offices. In the employment market they also enjoyed certain priorities. At the time, rumors floated around that Volkswagen was exploring the possibility of an assembling plant in Ethiopia. The Emperor had insisted that Asmara was an excellent venue; after all, look at Unilever. The company chose Asmara for its detergent and soap factory. Asmara hosted the most significant international exhibition in those days. And yet the Eritrean students carried resentment around with them. Was that based on mistreatment? I can profoundly say, no.

There were agitators, all with their own agendas to push. The Islamic group, "El Jebeha," originated in Morocco and in the late 1960;s they became the Eritrean Liberation Front (ELF). The ELF was trained and financed by Syria and Libya. None of these countries share a border with Ethiopia, and yet, since the 1960s, they were causing trouble for Ethiopia in the north. There is no recorded historical animosity, no apparent common interest and no logical reason for armed conflict. Initially, it was banditry targeting trucks and vehicles in peaceful regions where people moved freely between Asmara and Addis Ababa, causing the movement to be dangerous, especially near Keren.

The desire to separate Eritrea as a Muslim state might explain the rising of the Arab countries against Ethiopia to gain complete Arab control of the Red Sea, but Eritrea was not predominantly Muslim so all this unrest seemed so absurd to me. Eritrean students used their available finances, to buy sympathizers for their cause, whatever it may have been. External forces, whose financial interests would have been endangered by the path Ethiopia was following, instigated the problem. And for me, the identity of the instigators remains the unanswered question. Syria, Libya, and even Morocco paid dearly for their meddling in Ethiopia. They contributed to the program to dismantle Ethiopia; and suffered the same too. "He who lives by the sword dies by the sword. (Genesis 31)"

The territory on the Red Sea coast of Ethiopia was known as Bahere Negash. It had a loose autonomy, and because Ethiopian rulers avoided conflict with colonizing forces, they supported that status-quo, Eritreans ethnically, linguistically, and culturally have insignificant differences from their neighbors in Ethiopia. I have no sympathy for the Eritrean students of that time as they had no valid reasons to erupt in such violence. External forces coerced the Eritrean students to destabilize Ethiopia. I don't think they intended to create an independent Eritrea. It is impossible to pinpoint the agitators behind it, but my conviction is that the oil in the Ogaden had a lot to do with what was going on. Tenneco was exploring for oil at this time. Now, maybe it's just coincidence, but the positive reports of a significant find could have been the reason for the unrest of the students. During a survey, the Tenneco geologist and engineers were kidnaped by the ELF together with the helicopter pilot, with whom I had the pleasure to be acquainted with long after his experience. It was an international incident, which unfortunately attracted world media.

The media portrayed the image of Ethiopia to the world from an entirely different perspective, and the oil exploration and the talks about it subsided.

In the summer of 1973, as part of my engineering studies, I did an apprenticeship, which shortened my vacation time so I couldn't visit home. The previous year I had seen Addis Ababa at its highest peak ever in development, entertainment, and abundance of consumer goods and foodstuff. Also, it was around this time that weddings for my generation had begun. I defended the thesis for my masters on July 2, 1974, but stayed in Armenia an extra month to complete another project, one that I had promised to my uncle before his sudden death. The task was the completion or updating of the Vorperian family tree, and I would not dream of leaving before that promise was fulfilled.

The Khosrof Vorperian family, all of them very hospitable relatives, wanted me to visit regularly, but I found myself too busy with other things. The few times per term that I visited them, they were always so happy to have me there, being eager hosts. Often, the topic of conversation revolved around the family tree. They'd say that I would have to be the one to update the tree; after all, I was the one studying engineering. It was essential to them that I get the job done and that I include all the names collected. I kept promising, but I never followed through. Upon my return from Beirut in August 1973, I visited with Uncle Khosrof and his son Nishan, and again at the end of October, I saw them and another time in the middle of autumn, under a flowering tree that he planted years back. Uncle Khosrof took me to the tree and said, "do you see the blossom on this tree? Vartkes, it means I will die soon." Legend has it that the one who planted that tree will die if it blossoms during the autumn. Shaken by his words I dismissed him saying, "do not interfere in the affairs of God," and this prompted him to take both my arms in his hands and implore, "whatever happens Vartkes, promise that you will update the family tree." And only a few weeks later he drew his last breath. His death was a blow for me, and I to this day I still regret my lazy indifference in seeing his wish through to see a completed family tree before he died.

I stayed in Lebanon for three weeks, and on the 25th of August 1974, my cousin Eddie, his wife Diana and I boarded the plane to Addis Ababa. They updated me on the events of the beginning of the revolution in Ethiopia, in February that year.

I was about to enter the abyss of the unknown.

CHAPTER SEVEN

"Why Ethiopia?" meaning "how come Armenians came to Ethiopia?" I get this question all the time, no matter what the situation and no matter who is doing the interviewing. It is a question I must always answer.

It's a simple question, but it is not simple to answer. The Armenian presence in Ethiopia is engrossed in an eras-long history during which both nations shared many religious and historical ties. Ethiopians and Armenians have a natural kinship towards each other, based on the mutual understanding and co-operation between the two nations that had been developed over many centuries.

I will restrict myself to quoting a few historical remarks dating back to 451 AD.

In 451 AD, both Ethiopians and Armenians rejected the Chalcedonian Creed. Hence both belong to the family of The Oriental Orthodox Churches. In 1514 Queen Elleni sent the Armenian merchant Matheos as envoy to the court of King Manuel of Portugal. Other Armenian envoys also went to the Mogul Empire, France, and the Dutch East Indies representing different monarchies. Later, Boghos Markarian accompanied the envoys of Menelik to Egypt, and Sarkis Terzian brought munitions for Ethiopia before the Adua war and accompanied a diplomatic mission to Washington DC. Baghdasarian started the minting of the Menelik coins and initiated the monetary system of Ethiopia.

It was at Melkonian that I noticed how Armenians from other countries were supporting Abebe Bikila, an African who overtook

Emil Zatopek, a European, while watching a film of the 1960 Rome Olympics. It was not for our sake; I can tell you; it was purely a natural impulse. I felt the same sentiment amongst the Armenians in Yerevan.

And yet in the 1970s, Ethiopia grew intolerant of the Armenians. Fewer than 1500 Armenians were living in Ethiopia during that period, and amongst that small population, Armenians started to emigrate from Ethiopia towards a vast unknown which those of us who stayed found very shocking. It was more astounding to see that members of our immediate family were also packing their bags.

Before retelling of the uprooting of immediate family seeking a new life in a new country, to create a second diaspora of Ethiopian Armenians by this migration. A glimpse into the forging of the family in Ethiopia is worth mentioning.

For our family, it began in 1895 when my maternal grandmother's uncle, Hovsep Toroian, was invited to Ethiopia to design and develop the gardens of the palace. Back then, then, the situation under the reign of Sultan Abdul Hamid within the Ottoman Empire was becoming increasingly more intolerable for Armenians who were faced with constant harassments, rape, and massacre. Leaving Armenia for this commission was an attractive prospect that proposed the possibility of a better life.

Samuel Behesnilian, Hovsep's second brother, followed him there in 1902 upon completing his college education. Samuel was a shrewd businessman who in a short time secured enough savings to go back to Adana, where the family had settled after leaving Behesni. He convinced his parents Haroutioun and Trfanda to come to Ethiopia with them. The entire family moved to Ethiopia including his sister Ovsanna (my great-great-grandmother) who was married to Haroutioun Djerrahian. Their first child Vartouhi was born in Ethiopia in 1905.

Amid the political maneuvers of the superpowers, the United Kingdom, Germany and Austro-Hungary, France and Russia, "The Daily Mail" in 1902 assigned Roupen Vorperian (activist, poet, journalist, and photographer) to be stationed in Djibouti. The Russians had negotiated with China to take over Port Arthur, upsetting Japan. The British, who were allies with Japan, were closely monitoring the movement of the Russian navy. It was just before the Russo-Japanese war.

In letters home to his family, Malatia Roupen described the beauty of Ethiopia, the potential for a better life there and how magnanimous Emperor Menelik II was. My maternal grandfather Kevork Vorperian, a cousin to Roupen, together with his nephew, Artin, came to visit Djibouti during the summer of 1906. The unbearable heat of the summer had always been a reason for Roupen to pass the time in Harar with Yessayi Garigian, the owner of the first tannery in Ethiopia. Kevork and Artin from Harar proceeded to Addis Ababa, while Roupen returned to Djibouti. In 1924 Kevork married Vartouhi Djerrahian, and together they had seven children Marine, Elise, Assadour, Roupen, Ovsanna, Hovhannes (Onno) and Dikran.

In 1923, wife of then Regent Ras Teferi Mekonen, Itegue Menene, accompanied by Mrs. Araxie Yazedian went to Jerusalem. While there, they visited the Saint James Armenian Monastery where she came across a band of orphans. The following year her husband, Regent Teferi Mekonen detoured to Jerusalem on his way from Ethiopia. He was on his way to Geneva to represent Ethiopia at the League of Nations and then off to attend the Paris Olympics of 1924. What he saw in Jerusalem touched his heart and without hesitation, he invited the 40 orphans to come to Ethiopia.

At that same time, Kevork Nalbandian, labeled as a communist activist, left Aleppo escaping to Cairo. The AGBU (The Armenian General Benevolent Union) needed a bandmaster as their teacher and leader to accompany the fanfare to Ethiopia. Kevork Nalbandian and Father Hovhannes Simeonian together with the band arrived in Addis Ababa on the afternoon of 23 November 1924.

Kevork's older brother, my grandfather Haroutioun, followed his brother to Ethiopia in 1932. It seemed like a good idea after losing his job as an interpreter to the British contingency in Aleppo, and after several failed business ventures. The situation in the world was tense and communication between Addis Ababa and Aleppo very strained. It took him many years to arrange for his family to join him in Ethiopia, but finally, during the Italian occupation in 1938 my grandmother, Nartouhi, along with her children Nerses, Marie, Hrant, and Puzant arrived in Addis Ababa. Nerses married Elise Vorperian, on the 7th of September 1947 and had four children Hermine, Vartkes, Salpi, and Harout.

Every family had a good reason to come or some connection to Ethiopia, and this is how I came to be born in Ethiopia, calling it home.

And now, this family had started to separate and disperse. One of the first to leave was Uncle Manuel, who was married to my Aunt Ovsanna; they left to London, England. Uncle Manuel was a successful entrepreneur with a strong and supportive wife, and they integrated quickly into English society.

Nartouhi Karibian née Vorperian, the daughter of Artin Vorperian, was the first to pack up everything and go to Australia. It could not have been the baptism of her youngest son Vicken, born in Ethiopia, as I was in Armenia at the time, but there was an occasion at he house, when I remember her saying that we should all move out of Ethiopia. Things were going bad and were only going to get worse. She worked in UNICEF or at least she had joined UNICEF when she first joined the United Nations and perhaps with her access to the educated elite of ethnic Ethiopians; she was privy to more information than we were. Upon my return from University, they were already gone.

After living 50 years in Ethiopia Uncle Hrant together with the family moved to Adelaide, Australia. Hrant was denied citizenship several times, as, he was labeled a communist just like Uncle Kevork. Hrant was patriotic and keenly interested in the development of Soviet Armenia, and he told anyone concerned about the events there. It was all about Armenia and not the political system in Soviet Armenia. Uncle Hrant was, directly and indirectly, instrumental in seeing that over 30 Armenian youngsters from Ethiopia received their higher education. If it were not for Armenia, most of them would not have had the opportunity for a degree or a successful career. He was an intelligent person with strong convictions and had an extraordinary premonition about the future of Ethiopia; all of which proved to be accurate. Uncle Hrant left Ethiopia on an emergency travel document. On my return, they too were gone.

Uncle Onno was lingering around when I arrived in Addis Ababa in 1974, waiting for the verdict regarding his shares. Onno was born in Ethiopia where he studied and worked. A graduate of Teferi Mekonen school he had to cut his studies short in the Haile Selassie I University to support the family. He too was an intelligent, shrewd businessman.

Their departures affected me profoundly, and my heart became heavy in dismay over the dispersion of the family. The dwindling numbers of the community depressed me as I understood the great sacrifices made by our elders to up and leave their lives to start new lives here. I couldn't understand their reasons for the up-rooting to restart a new struggle all over again. Armenians are not economic migrants who seek a better prospect for their business. Wherever they lived, that was the motherland, and Ethiopia was the motherland for the Ethio-Armenians. They were actual citizens of Ethiopia, and even with the rejections of their citizenship, they felt Ethiopian. Armenians earned and built in Ethiopia; they had no intention of moving. What did they see that we did not?

Armenians were no longer in the palace or in essential government posts; we had nothing to arouse the envy of the ethnic Ethiopians. The Armenians were in the piazza and around the Armenian club. They were there because when they came, there was nothing in Addis Ababa. Armenians together with their brotherly Ethiopian people, built Addis Ababa.

During an interview, university students asked me how the Armenians had acquired centrally located properties in Addis Ababa. My reply was "when they were given the land as payment for their work, it wasn't prime real estate because all there was in Addis Ababa was empty land." And, regarding the stone houses in Filweha Meda belonging to the 40 lidjoch (orphans), it was given to them as part of the agreement to come to Ethiopia. That land was marshland that the Armenians cleared. And now these historic houses are under threat because of new development without any regard for the history and lives that are being uprooted.

Instead of paying money to the Armenians who served him, Emperor Menelik II compensated them by giving them plots of land. Boghos Markarian got a piece of land in Arat Kilo, Dikran Ebeyan across from the Armenian school, Hagop Baghdassarian near Sidist Kilo, Krikorios Boghossian, near St Mary's Cathedral. Against the bridges that he built Krikor Hovian got the site of the Saint Kevork church and the area next to Arba Dereja. He cut down part of the land that was given to him to construct the forty step staircase for public use.

These land allocations also have another significance. Emperor Menelik's palace was surrounded by lands, which were occupied by his statesmen, up to the rivers. Across the rivers, it was allocated to the employees, and thus part of it was called "Serategna Sefer" meaning worker's quarters. No one could cross the river as there was no bridge. The lands in between that had been given to Armenians strategically buffered these two areas. Armenians were loyal subjects to Menelik and not slaves to Menelik with stamps on their backsides as the malicious rumors were circulating. On the contrary, Menelik recognized, appreciated and valued the Armenian community in response to the loyalty Armenians showed. And no one was branded as such.

And there were Armenians who took up arms for Emperor Menelik, and later for Emperor Haile Selassie against the Fascist regime and there were those who lost their lives in battle.

Despite all this at the peak of Ethiopia's development, the Armenians started leaving.

CHAPTER EIGHT

> Without any blood
> The wicked vanquish
> With a good devotion
> Let Ethiopia flourish

The sonorous words of the Revolution Anthem haunted the atmosphere. It had meaning initially, but on the 23rd of November 1974 it became a farce; blood was in the air. It was a Sunday. We were driving back from Metahara. Upon reaching the outskirts of Addis Ababa, we noticed the red sky, and I do not mean metaphorically. A deep shiver coursed through me; the atmosphere was scary. People regarded the reddening of the sky as the blood reflected in it. The blood of the sixty highly placed individuals, assassinated in prison, without any trial. A few of them had held office only recently. And one was General Michael Andom, who was the first chairman of the Derg. Though we thought those were the evil and harmful ones we were about to learn that the wicked terror was yet to come.

And on the radio, the smug voice of the announcer shattered the cold crimson atmosphere of the morning. The orotund announcement called out the names, one by one by one, of those executed in the darkness of night — a cowardly act against unarmed people; a blemish on humanity.

The students and their agitators were proud, but what they failed to learn in history class was that instigators are often the first ones eliminated. The opportunists from Europe and within Ethiopia were aiming towards the palace, but they had miscalculated the fast trigger of the man whom "Newsweek" or "Time" magazines praised as the strongman behind the scene some months earlier while praising Mengistu Haile Mariam. How did the foreign journalists know about him? It amazed me.

The BBC strongly publicized the hunger in Wollo, to the extent that the word Ethiopia was connected with famine, and according to their estimation a population of a hundred thousand was exposed to it. Famine was a useful tool for the revolutionaries to help popularize anti-government sentiments and they were able to whip the masses into a frenzy and achieve their goal. After the revolution, the famine spread and millions perished The revolution and the change of government could not solve the problem. Millions of lives lost to starvation, and instead of curtailing the terrible hunger, it increased its fifty-fold, reaching epidemic levels. How does a whole world watch and do nothing? Did these journalists feel proud of their accomplishment? Or were they serving the perpetrators who wanted Ethiopia's decline? Instead of placing their attention on negative propaganda, if they had used their power to feed the starving, there would be no destitution in Ethiopia today. Only their conscience can judge or torment them.

The revolution was triggered unexpectedly and without any preparation in February 1974, when the government was forced to increase the fuel price by Birr 0.10/per liter. The taxis called a strike, accompanied by the university students. Within a few days, the government gave in and reduced the price. But the revolution had already ignited. The agitators and the intellectuals or the so-called educated elite embraced the military. A committee of 100 individuals from different backgrounds was chosen to negotiate with the government. The committee later adopted the name Derg surely suggested by the intellectuals, who were unearthing new words from Ge'ez (The old language of Ethiopia), as from the military there were not many who had that level of education.

Without any resistance, government ministers, army generals, and other high-ranking officials gave themselves up. They probably believed that the Emperor held a trump card and could reverse the course, but that was not the case. The Derg had another plan for the Emperor. They chose a Volkswagen beetle and pushed the elderly monarch into the back seat and drove him to the headquarters of the fourth army division. From there they transferred him to an underground cell designated for him, within the Menelik Gibbi (The Menelik Palace Compound). The cell was probably under the office of Mengistu Hailemariam, who liked to boast that he sat over the grave of the imperialists. He could not distinguish the difference between the word emperor and imperialist.

The first three months there was a power struggle within the Derg. They were busy paving the way for eliminating each other. Consequently, groups with socialistic ideas developed in the cafés of Paris, showed the Derg the path to take. It displeased the West. The U.S. cut off the supply of weapons, spare parts, and ammunition for the old arsenal of Ethiopia and the Derg started shifting towards the U.S.S.R. Leonid Brezhnev who would not have minded a new ally in East Africa.

My brother Harout who had formed a band consisting of our sister, Salpi, Dikran Avakian and Vahan Djerrahian (I joined them upon my return), used to perform for events. We were playing at the "Juventus" Italian Club of Addis Ababa on New Year's Eve. Because there was curfew midnight to dawn, we would play overnight. Since the day I arrived in Addis in August the lockdown was in place, sometimes from nine to morning or ten to sunrise; the Derg needed the darkness of the night for their "development." It was dangerous to be be out during restricted hours, because it was shoot first, ask questions later. On the eve of 1975, precisely at midnight, there was the horrifying sound that usually indicated a new action, a proclamation or extermination. Awaiting news of another elimination, we were dumbfounded to hear that this time it was sounded to announce the Nationalization of the financial institutions, the bank and the insurance companies. In the morning going home, happy faces on the streets were cheering us, with big smiles. The wording of the announcement implied that these institutions had sucked the blood of the poor and now those became the property of the broad masses.

At a certain point, banknotes changed. It was before or after the nationalization of the financial institutions, I cannot say for sure. Again, that horrific single noted rhythmic music played in unison with few instruments out of tune. It made your heart beat faster. The money by an imperialist government was improved, that meant the currency bore a new inscription, "legal tender in Ethiopia," indicating it was now a valueless paper, but it belonged to the people, and they penalized the "hoarders" who lost 8% on the 100 and 50-bill notes. The propaganda machine announced this as a great victory.

On 3 February 1975, I could hear from neighbors' radios, the dreadful sound again and the ensuing announcement that followed. This time it was the nationalization of the industries. The foreign community and the Armenians were stricken. I did not catch the wording of the nationalization, as I received a call at exactly that moment from my friend Antranig whose wife Ashkhen also a friend, was going to give birth. It was a two-minute drive from our house to theirs, so I rushed them to the hospital. A few hours later they had their twins. In the evening I watched the televised broadcast to catch the narrative of the nationalization. "The capitalist bloodsucking embezzlers" was the title of the industrialists on this occasion. It shook the Armenian community to the core from the 72 names announced 12 belonged purely to Armenians, and many Armenians had shares in other nationalized industries. The Italians and the Greeks after a few years received compensation, but the Armenians did not. To date, Ethiopians who lost industries did not get any payment, and many Armenians lived through the agony of seeing their efforts sold to third parties.

Thus, began an era of betrayal and backstabbing; husbands against their wives, wives against husbands, children against parents, partners against each other and colleagues against one another. The loss was devastating causing conflict between people where before there was none. The one day in February, the grim voice of Uncle Puzant's employee, Tilahun, over the phone informed us that

"I Want to Die with a Flag"

the security police have impounded the shop and taken uncle to the 3rd police station or rather the notorious "Mehakelawi" for further questioning. My father and I rushed there to understand the reasons for his arrest. It was top secret. The few persons we contacted the answer we heard was - it's a grave matter - and no one wanted to give any information. On our way out from the compound a policeman who recognized us looked at a lady arriving, then back at us and told us. "Ask her. She knows." A few weeks later in the courtroom, we understood the meaning of this comment.

Uncle Puzant was accused of "Economic Sabotage." The investigators had found the foreign bank account with the address in the diary of an American businessman who lived in Ethiopia for quite a long time. The courtroom was in a gloomy room in the Menelik palace compound and the presiding judge, Colonel Belay Negga, in his military uniform looked elegant, impressive and severe. The three prisoners entered, and the prosecutor presented the case. The judge asked, "guilty or not guilty." Upon their "not guilty" reply he adjourned the case for three days for our response. We had no previous run-ins with the law and no court experience, so we had nothing else to do but put our trust in the lawyer, referred by acquaintances. The lawyer was seemingly very bright and educated, and he assured us that everything would be fine. On the third day, in the courtroom the lawyer was silent. He did not try to defend. When we poked him, he said he would do it during cross-examination. He did nothing during cross-examination either.

The American businessman was acquitted and had to leave Ethiopia within 48 hours. The other man was given a suspended sentence because his lawyer presented a case that the livelihood of many ethnic Ethiopians depended on him. And Uncle Puzant, whose only crime was that he had USD 64.00 in a foreign bank was sentenced to four years of rigorous imprisonment. It was the remnanat of the money he had transferred before he became an Ethiopian citizen four years earlier. And Uncle Hrant was convicted for five years, whose crime was that he had USD 458. Hrant who was denied the Ethiopian citizenship had the right to have money abroad as a foreigner. I was going to start my new job in May, but until then I looked after my uncle's shop.

The gross injustice of citizenship was infuriating. We were Ethiopians, and yet, we were not. We were not given equal and fair treatment; instead, they made examples of us. For punishment, I guess we were Ethiopian enough but not for everything.

I joined Bulvinos Chemicals a British Company which supplied chemicals to different industries in Ethiopia. After a few weeks of training I started visiting the customers who were already buying from the company and those, who were potential customers. The newly Nationalized factories were active, and there was a lot of enthusiasm within the management around replenishing stock. It was a good start for me. Being a science student all my scholastic years the commercial terms were a novelty to me. In the evenings I studied the terms of international business from the books I purchased, making good use of the curfew.

One of my first tests was with a textile company. This company would have had to stop production within 30 days as they were running short of caustic soda and could not borrow from other factories. They called a few suppliers and asked if we could bring in the caustic soda within the specified time. All said it was impossible, but I asked for a day to reply. The next day I confirmed that if I had the purchase order in hand immediately, I'd be able to make it happen. At the time, the Suez Canal was closed, and the goods were shipped either via Aqaba by through the "land-bridge" or via the cape. Within 23 days I had 100 tons of caustic soda in Assab and flew there to have the goods loaded on trucks. On the 26th day after the order, the products were in their store. Our company became a favored supplier until the government introduced a purchasing system by government tender. It was one of the first reasons factories started to fail.

The morning of May 7, 1975, again we awoke to the horrific music, that signals trouble, this time to news of the nationalization of the houses. It was a piece of alarming news. It was the most inhumane, controversial and unconstitutional decree, which is still in effect today. The nationalization of so-called "extra houses" in today's market, where individuals and families own many multifloored villas and skyscrapers, is discriminatory and unfair to say the least. In short, the proclamation declared that any dwelling rented out is an "extra" house, and as of that date it becomes public property. However, the owners could choose one of the houses if they had more than one but had to move to the house of their choice within six months. Our house in "Arat Kilo" was an interconnected two-floor house. To avoid the "Dr. Zhivago" scenes of others being brought into our lives, we chose our home in Bole and following the proclamation we gave notice to "Total" to vacate the house within six months.

Only a few foreigners righteous enough were ready to leave the house within six months. All the embassies and diplomats who occupied significant dwellings did not cooperate with the owners, and the government supported them. The embassies and international organizations, with their action, endorsed an inhumane law to secure personal tranquility. A month before the due date our father, a respected celebrity in Ethiopia was denied entry to the Total manager's office by a secretary. But revenge came soon enough.

The Derg, the defenders of the poor, once out of the military barracks, had started to acquire the taste for luxury while playing in the houses of the assassinated nobleman. But to use these properties would have attracted criticism, so instead, they targeted properties, which were not very recognizable. They issued an internal memorandum (which later was called a directive) according to which houses over 180 square meters would not be returned to the owners, even if it was their only house. Fikreselassie Wogderess the third person in command chose ours in Bole, and they threw out Total within a week. The same manager who kicked out our father from his office had to take whatever was available. "God acts in mysterious ways." Still to this day I hesitate to go into a Total petrol station.

In August 1975, the Urban Dwellers Association was formed by the government. The first thing they did was to collect a census of the houses. A group of five people brought out a prepared questionnaire and forms to be filled numbered 003 and 004. 004 meant that you own the house it is your chosen house. 003 indicated the extra property. The Arat Kilo house was not our house of choice; therefore, we got the 003 forms. They decided that it was suitable for multi-family use as it had four toilets. So, we got two numbers 209 and 210. We were allowed to live in rent-free on the upper floor, against the Bole dwelling. But as suspected, the neighbors wanted to rent the ground floor of our Arat Kilo house where my grandmother lived. Strangers were going to co-habit in a house which had one electricity meter, one water meter, and one telephone line with multiple sockets. It would have been worse than the Dr. Zhivago house. For 39 years, I paid land tax and rent to the government for the family house that was built by my father and mother and even though the decree explicitly states that the government will pay compensation against the nationalized houses this has not happened. It would be a gross understatement to say that this is frustrating, but legally it is expropriation, as there is nothing a person can do to see that the government complies with their own statements. The government at its convenience enforces or ignores this inhumane proclamation up to this date.

The twin of our Arat Kilo house, which used to belong to Artin Vorperian, received multiple numbers during the census. The underground which had an external door unlike ours and the three rooms of the service quarters received separate numbers. Initially, there were tenants whom we knew for quite some time; these were young secretaries who co-shared the first and second floor. The underground and the services were briefly rented out. Later the whole house was converted to some general government office, prison, interrogation center, vote counting facility and served many functions. The unfortunate thing was that we shared the compound for about a year.

The Bishoftu resort was deemed an "extra" house, so we had to deliver it to the kebele officially, which assigned someone to do an inventory of the house, counting light bulbs, doors and windows, remarking on a cracked window glass, as if it was their property that we had mishandled. Upon returning there sixteen years later, there was no house (just the floor tiles remained being baked in the sun), no orchard, no vegetable garden, and the precious rose garden with over fifty different types of roses had disappeared. The stones of the terraces and the surrounding wall of the land were taken and used by others to build houses. The swimming pool filled with rocks and the pump in the lake was considered unnecessary and dismantled. It was empty land when our father bought the place, and it sat in ruins and arid land when we saw it again. That was living proof of "development under government management."

My father wanted to rent the house, like Uncle Elias, whose summer house was next to ours, but the reply was a definitive no. Later rumors reached us that one of the officers had rented it for himself. After a few months, when he had realized that he could not maintain the place on his teacher's salary, he abandoned the site, making sure that the counted bulbs along with the holders traveled with him.

The academic year was almost over, but the government did not wait to disperse the students, the propaganda and the brainwashing machine was as powerful as the Nazi Germany propaganda setup. The students voluntarily took responsibility to teach the broad masses to read and write, within six months. There was a procession for their departure, and a big choir was amassed to perform for that farewell. We were considered part of the bourgeoisie, so instead of asking our father to prepare the choir, they tried with many other musicians. Finally, they called our father to take charge of it. The deadline was too short; he worked day and night and prepared four fabulous chorales and taught the group of 250 students. He was summoned to conduct the choir at the Meskel square, or the renamed Revolution Square, from where the students went into the buses towards the interior. The students who stirred up trouble succeeded in disrupting the university which never reached that peak again. Many perished from malaria and other diseases unknown in Addis Ababa, and many of them escaped, starting the

Ethiopian Diaspora. Others created the base of armed struggle, eventually toppling the Derg.

The Derg decided to change the National Anthem, They could have changed the wording especially the one phrase praising the king, "let our king live for our honor," but instead they wanted a new one as if Ethiopia had not existed before their era. There was an announcement of a competition in the newspapers, but our father, who didn't believe in changing the anthem and he expected there to be a controversy if he won, so he decided not to participate. The committee had not been able to make a selection, so a new announcement was published, with an addition of something to effect of "all musicians living in Ethiopia are asked to participate."

The Poet Laureate Tsegaye Gebremedhin came over to our house and asked our father to compose the music to his poem; our father told Tsegaye it's better to ask an ethnic musician to produce the music, as his would not be accepted. Tsegaye insisted that the times are different. Our father agreed. At the same time, the National Theatre (the renamed Haile Selassie I Theatre) also decided to participate in the contest. Two anthems by my father were recorded and submitted to the committee. Both hymns composed by my father had passed the requirements, and so he was invited to the palace. Major Atnafu Abate, the second man in command, received him. It was a rainy day, my was in a raincoat and furry hat (merely a coincidence) purchased a decade ago in Moscow. Atnafu Abate congratulated our father and told him to prepare for a trip to Moscow to conduct the famous Soviet Military band and record the new National Anthem of Ethiopia.

The controversy surfaced immediately. Upon the instigation of a mediocre musician in the army, whose narrow-minded nationalism had fueled his envy, or vice-versa, he'd been able to convince the junta that a second Nalbandian should not be the author of the new anthem. At this point an Armenian was not an Ethiopian. Fifteen days later my father was told that his music was too advanced for a developing country. They wanted him to join the committee to choose a more unadorned anthem presented by the next contestants.

Daniel, (I do not remember his father's name) was the winner, but the recording of the music was not to be in Moscow. After some corrections by our father, upon the request of the author, the music was played. Daniel had written a letter to our father accepting and allowing the corrections.

Laureate Tsegaye Gebremedhin, to whom our father had told what happened was more shocked by this than anyone else.

In June, the government nationalized the rural land. The chanted motto of the students "farmland to the tiller" vanished in thin air. The land became the property of the masses but became inaccessible to everyone, paving the way to corruption.

The last group of the students that included the twelve grade graduates were seen off on the first anniversary of the revolution. Our father conducted the choir at Revolution Square.

The exodus of the Armenians intensified, particularly after the nationalization of the houses, as it meant they lost all their life savings and old age security. They emigrated to Australia, Canada, and the United States of America. Even the pastor, who was ordained for our church but had nothing in Ethiopia left for the U.S.A. Reverend Vahan Topalian came to serve, but the community council decided to dismiss him even though he was seen to be an asset to the community at that crucial time. The committee itself depleted and only three out of the seven elected persons remained. Everybody left without saying goodbye or transferring community papers to anyone; no one knew about the movement of the other. Many aspects of the community were falling apart as community leaders became secretive and usually, only after a family's departure did we hear about it. The secrecy made sense since many people were returned from the airport because the house helps, for additional severance pay and compensation, created havoc at the airport and the departing family was denied entry to the terminal until the matter was resolved. Most Armenians left their shops and businesses to their employees.

The Sevan Band, established by our brother Harout, gave probably its last performance in the Addis Ababa stadium, in a concert aimed at collecting money for the famine fund. It was an excellent performance. Through our father's work, we had contacts with musicians who came to Ethiopia. The renowned jazz musician's saxophonist Hal Singer, bassist Jimmy Woode, pianist Horace Partan and a percussionist whose name alas I cannot recall all spent an afternoon at our house together with Harout playing his guitar. It was a memorable afternoon, that paved the way for Harout to go to Berklee College of Music in Boston. Our father had also written a recommendation, specifying the talent of his son. Harout left for the U.S.A. to pursue a musical career, the only one from the family to follow in our father's footsteps. The next year he came to Ethiopia and got engaged to his girlfriend, Seza Mekhdjian. Obtaining an exit visa was becoming more difficult, but we were lucky. I wrote a simple application; we went to immigration and got the permit within two days. The citizenship issue had also affected Harout, as he faced difficulties at Beirut airport, but at least for him being stateless was helpful to leave Ethiopia without a big hassle.

During the last three months of 1976, there was increased activity in our house. The traditional instrument of the musicians from Asosa was being modified and tuned by our father so that the sounds would integrate nicely with that of the orchestras. The National Theatre and musicians from all over Ethiopia were preparing for the Festac 1977. At this time the air of racism had calmed, and the government wanted Ethiopia to show something spectacular, and so they admitted that they needed my father's contribution. They sent him to Lagos as an Ethiopian musician. It was a first and a last for Ethiopia. Before the Festac in January 1977 our father went to the hospital for a prostatectomy. In Nigeria, he felt weak and left the festival within five days, to come home.

CHAPTER NINE

One day as I was stopped at a red light at Meskel Square on my way towards Akaki, I heard someone call my name. It was my old kindergarten friend Mary Sakadjian in the passenger seat of the car next to me. Before we could exchange hellos, but not before she handed me her business card, the light turned green. They headed left towards the airport, and I continued straight. It was not the first time we bumped into each other. We had several times before, briefly, in my friend John's father's shop. John's sister Emma and Mary were close friends.

I used to travel to Bahir Dar, Dire Dawa and Asmara for business quite often, and I started to purchase the airline tickets from ETTA, where Mary worked, and through that, our friendship grew. I often visited her at the office and would sometimes confide that my relationship with my current girlfriend was shaky. She used to write twice-weekly letters and soon they were reduced to once a month and shortly thereafter, she had stopped writing altogether. Then, on May 9, 1976, Mary and I had a fabulous time dancing together at a wedding all night long. At one point, I even had her feather boa around my neck, which was the subject of some gossip within the Armenian Community. But we were just good friends. When my mother asked me, what was going on between Mary and me, that's exactly what I told her, "nothing. We're friends."

I worked with a man named Vartan Ouzounian and one night he had asked me to invite Mary to dinner before his trip out of Ethiopia on September 6, 1976. The night before Vartan left Mary called me up to say that her mother had just passed away and she asked me to help her with the church proceedings since she and her brothers had no idea how to handle such a situation. I went to her house and explained in detail what was required. I promised to arrange everything needed in the church and the cemetery. Also, I informed them that an Armenian cleric, Reverend Nerseh Papudjian from Paris, was in town for a meeting and that he would perform the funeral service for her mother, and I arranged that for them too.

As is customary amongst the Armenian people and Ethiopians as well, I waited forty days to invite her to dinner. In the interim, I liked to go to see her at the office and sometimes drive her to her house. That New Year's Eve I wanted to invite her to the Hilton, where we would be celebrating with the Chorbadjians, who left Ethiopia shortly after. This would be the last time the whole group the Chorbadjians, Aslanians, and Nalbandians would be together. I deliberated for a long time and came very close to asking her to join me but then thought better of it. Knowing how grief-stricken she was over the passing of her mother, it would have been too difficult for her to attend a ball only three months later. Instead of inviting her, I gave her a New Year's gift, and with my best wishes, pulled myself away from her office that day, silently wishing she could have been with me that night.

Mary's grief subsided, and she started to get back to making plans, organizing dinners and providing a medium for baking such wonderful treats by Mr. Freddie Stordiau who was a guest in the Sakadjian household during some difficult challenges he was facing. Under blackmail, Mr. Stordiau had been forced to sell his house to the housing administration at a ridiculously low price. Freddie was the son of one of the first bakers of Ethiopia. His cake creations were masterpieces; except for his heavy hand in adding liquor to the mix. One invitation that Mary extended to us (my parents were included) was to introduce her older brother to my older sister. My father was sick in bed and couldn't come, but when we arrived home later that night, my mother said, "I understand what Mary was trying to do, but what about the two of you?" She saw something between us, but she accepted my reply that we were good friends.

"I Want to Die with a Flag"

I received an unexpected call from Mr. Stordiau; he wanted to see me. The next day I went to see him at the Sakadjian residence, and after a long talk, he wanted to know if I was serious about Mary with all my flirting. He told me that Mary had other plans; ones that didn't include me. I replied to him what I told everyone else who asked, "Mary and I are just good friends." And then he cautioned me to keep the meeting a secret from her. I left thinking and analyzing the meeting, which did not make any sense to me as Mary, who was an open and honest person, would have told me of her plans. The next two days I distanced myself from Mary, and then I received a call close to the end of office hours from her. An Ethiopian family friend had seen my car in front of the house during office hours and scolded her that she should not entertain me when her brothers are not home. I told her about my conversation with Mr. Stordiau (against his cautioning me not to). She said, "come pick me up." Her brothers and Mr. Stordiau were there when we arrived. She insisted I stay for a drink, and so I did. After chatting a bit, I was ready to leave and said my goodbyes, and that's when Mary pecked me on the cheek with a goodnight kiss. This was the first time for us to show any physical affection in front of the others, (or at all) and although it was not intimate, there were multiple messages in our first public kiss. Ironically, following that kiss, there was tension between us for a couple of weeks.

And one day, the worst kind of news came to me about Mary. An Armenian friend who was buying a ticket from Mary told me that she had seen a security guard take her away to the palace. When people are taken to the "Gibbi" for questioning they all too often disappeared altogether or remained indefinitely in the fourth army division headquarters, waiting for an amnesty on the anniversary of the revolution on September 12. Frantic, the first thing I did was to inform her brothers, and then we rushed to her office where her boss, Genna Desta also in a total panic, was trying desperately to understand what grounds they could have possibly had to take her away. I told him to let me know as soon as he knew something and whatever the outcome was.

Early in the afternoon, they brought her to the office looking for the evidence, claiming that Mary had cooperated with counter-revolutionaries. They made this claim because she issued the travel ticket to someone who killed a noble revolutionary or someone of some importance. They showed her the photo of a young military officer and claimed that they had evidence that she sent the tickets to two Ethiopians. Further, the Organization of African Unity (OAU) had ordered MCO's (Miscellaneous Charges Order), covering the cost of flights for two from Nairobi to Khartoum and that she had issued the MCO's to the order of the OAU. Mary had no clue who these people were and was not complicit, but Atnafu Abate insisted that she co-operated with counter-revolutionaries.

The person in charge of the travel plans in the OAU, Ambassador Ellie Dingha confirmed and proved to the Ethiopian Authorities, that it was the OAU who sent the tickets and not Mary. One of the lucky ones, Mary was released. Years later when the government banned sales of airline tickets by travel agencies, while Mary was going through the files, she found out that one of the MCO's issued to the OAU was for Issayas Afeworki, the leader of EPLF who became the first president of Eritrea after its independence in 1993.

To most of our friends, we were a couple even though neither of us admitted it. When Mary's friends invited her over, they always included me in their invitations. We attended fabulous parties together, which gave me serenity and took my mind off the declining health of my father. He had always been a healthy person, but right after the operation removing his prostate, his health deteriorated. Arshavir Terzian used to come to the house and take his blood for analysis; for him, it was clear that it was hepatitis of the liver. At the time there were no antigens to determine the strain of the hepatitis virus like there is now. Dr. Anna, Dr. Kevork (our cousin) his wife Dr. Adelina all came out of his room gloomy; they knew, as did we that there was something seriously wrong with him.

Arakel, Mary's older brother and my sister Hermine got engaged, which brought a moment of joy to our father. We decided to evacuate him to London to meet with other doctors. All the appointments with top specialists secured, hospital rooms reserved, his medical exit visa arranged, late October our father left Ethiopia with our mother. Mary was there to see them off, and that was when I heard the last words my father would speak to me; my father told me, "she is a nice person Vartkes, and she will be good for you son." As he made his way down the stairs of Arat Kilo house, he took a long, lingering look back, as if he knew it would be the last time seeing the house – the home he made and the legacy that he built with great sacrifice – for the love of his family. He was only sixty-two.

On the 10th November Jirayr Ouzounian called to tell me that my father was not doing well, and the next day Vartan called to say he passed away. The final diagnosis made by the specialists in London was "non-alcoholic Cirrhosis." A few years later Arsho told me, not that there could be any treatment but with today's antigens, we would have diagnosed your father's disease as Hepatitis B. He said my father had contracted the virus through the blood transfusion after his prostatectomy.

The arrangements took a few days for the return of his remains, which was his wish, our wish and the wish of the Ethiopian public and the musicians. It was a hard week with hundreds of mourners coming to the house. The mourners and thousands of his students crowded the Bole airport, Mary was busy clearing the corpse, and we were waiting for my mother with whom a young novice reverend Vigen Aykazian (he is an archbishop now) accompanied her from London to Addis Ababa her to do the funeral service. There was a crowd in the thousands, who all followed us to the house, where the National Theatre Funeral Association (Idir) had set up a tent anticipating a big group, to accommodate everyone. In the evening the coffin was transferred to the church, where he had served 39 years as choirmaster. That was also his home.

The funeral was a state affair with me as the deacon of that church who assisted during all services. I stood in the first row beside the coffin of my father, something that I never imagined would happen so soon. It was hard to imagine Saint Kevork Church without its maestro. I had so much more to learn from him. The journey to the cemetery in Gulele, which was usually a 20 minutes' drive back then, took well over an hour until the last cars reached the cemetery. There were eulogies by the Armenian Community, the National Theatre, The Ministry of culture, The Ministry of Education, the Police and others that I do not remember. It was the lengthiest funeral that I had ever attended, and I have been to many. Friday evening, we planned for a holy mass. We had to break the ice and the sooner, the easier it would be. In the end, the whole church was in tears. Hermine and Salpi took over our father's position, and I, in front of the altar continued the services.

That New Year's Eve, my Aunt Mary invited us for dinner. I dropped Mary home from work, went up to wish her brothers a Happy New Year as they were both getting ready to go to a program of their own. Mary planned to remain home alone that night, but it was at the peak of the Red Terror, so I urged her to come with me, and she accepted. We enjoyed dinner at my aunt's and just before the midnight curfew we set out for home. Despite the sound of gunfire, we ventured into the fifteen-minute drive to her house. I counted 52 bodies along the way, and by the time we reached her home, we saw two more not far from her house. Her brothers could not come back after this hour, so I kept her company till dawn when we could move. I did not count, but I saw a few more bodies the short drive from her house to mine.

There was an estrangement in our relationship in February. It was a Saturday evening, and I wanted to invite her out. I noticed Sieglinde's car outside and indicating that Mary had other plans. Hesitantly I rang the bell, and her brother Benon opened the door, and when I went up to the living room, Mary barely greeted me, she could hardly look me in the eyes, but when I cornered her, she said that she had made up her mind and she would be leaving for the U.S. I left the house and returned to my car thinking, I love her, but I never told her. I drove away and saw them in my rearview mirror driving behind me. In Arat Kilo we separated I turned left, and they turned right. After a few hundred meters I knew I had procrastinated too long and decided that I had to say something before it was too late. I had to stop her before they reached the Italian Embassy, where I guessed there was a party. I started chasing them, and after the German Embassy, I blocked Sieglinde's car. Sieglinde seeing my rage, in her Austrian accent told me, "tell her whatever you are going to say, do not involve me." It was an awkward place and an awkward moment, but I proposed to Mary, and she came to my car and to my relief and excitement, she said yes.

I told my mother. The date for Arakel and Hermine's wedding was after Easter 1978, early May in Ethiopia (Ethiopia follows the Julian calendar). I told my mother that we want a small ceremony, but she said no and came up with the bright idea of a double wedding.

We were legally married with the civil service at the municipality of Addis Ababa on the 13th of May 1978 and we got married in church on the 21st day of May 1978. The reception was at the Addis Ababa Hilton, with over 500 guests. Hermine and Mary exchanged homes.

The officiating priest at our wedding, whom we invited from Lebanon, belonged to the Holy See of Cilicia, where our church is within the Holy See of Echmiadzin. Serving the church, we requested from our Archbishop in Cairo to send a priest or to come himself to officiate, but he could not travel at the time and had no one available in Cairo whom he could assign, so with our initiatives we had the priest from Beirut. This action created concern in Echmiadzin, who immediately sent Reverend Daniel Shamlian to Ethiopia. Despite all our efforts to please him, he could not acclimatize himself in Ethiopia, and within eighteen months left for England

We faced personal tragedies and upheaval, and due to the unsettled Ethiopian politics, this entwined our lives. The years 1976 to 1978 we had shared sorrow and joy amidst the ugly period of the red terror.

CHAPTER TEN

Any analysis regarding the period of the Red Terror which followed the revolution is beyond my scope. Besides, during the era of the supposed formation of these opposition groups, I was not personally in Ethiopia between 1968 and 1974, so I will avoid commenting about that epoch. The first murmuring of the names EPRP (Ethiopian People's Revolutionary Party) and MEISON (All Ethiopia Socialist Movement, the Amharic abbreviation) began in late 1975. If these groups existed before, not too many people in Addis Ababa were aware of them. Perhaps the few founders and members were confined to Paris cafés or university dormitories, working underground for the parties that wanted to dismantle Ethiopia.

My memories of the beginning of the Red Terror date back to the day when Major Mengistu Hailemariam showed gymnastics on the television, to prove his wellbeing. They had tried to assassinate him by ambushing his car. If I am not mistaken, he was always in a convoy, and nobody could identify which car he was in. Right after this event, they stormed houses and checked them thoroughly, even confiscating air-guns. The checking was so thorough that no one could get away with hiding a gun. So, whatever weapon was in the hands of the EPRP or MEISON as far as I can reason, had to be distributed by the military. It was neither ideological nor class struggle; it was a pure power struggle, a fast track to what they thought would be a better life. Nobody cared about the hungry in Wollo, not even the BBC. It seemed the famine had served a purpose. The next time we would hear of it again would be in 1982, when millions were at risk of starvation, suffering and dying.

The history of Ethiopia has been rewritten several times, by Ethiopian and foreign historians throughout its history, and all to serve a purpose or a sovereign. The way Champollion deciphered the hieroglyphic without visiting Egypt, someone should do the same with Ethiopian history without seeing Ethiopia and talking to historians by decoding the existing accounts. The problem is authors are trying to find illumination for an enigma, which is called Ethiopia.

As the undisputed ruler of the country, Mengistu unleashed a bloody "Red Terror Campaign." He oversaw the establishment of the Workers' Party of Ethiopia in 1984, a new constitution for Ethiopia in 1986 and the election of himself as president in September 1987. He faced a rebellion in Tigray and Eritrea, the worst droughts and famines ever to afflict Ethiopia, an economy ruined by the forced nationalization of farms and housing, an exodus of entire populations, and coup attempts by enemies.

The second anniversary of the revolution on September 12, 1977 showed indications that things were not going as smoothly as the Derg had hoped. On that day, Major Mengistu Hailemariam had several bottles with red dye that he smashed to the ground, and he made sure to mention the Greeks and the Armenians while doing so. At that instance, there were probably fewer than a hundred Greeks and less than four hundred Armenians. It astonishes me up to now, in what context Mengistu managed to combine the Armenians and the Greeks with the Red Terror. The Derg took away everything that the Armenians had saved during a century of their existence in Ethiopia; the spilled blood meant that Mengistu also wanted some blood. Apart from their contributions creating jobs, bringing orchestral culture to the masses, introducing technology, and building houses for old age security, the Armenians did not involve themselves in the politics of the country. We were being stripped of everything, but they could not take our dignity.

The years referred to as "Red Terror," and "White Terror" were years of political assassinations and vendetta killings. The killing of the victims was "Redly" or "Whitely." The bottom line is mostly innocent people, tens of thousands of innocent civilians, who had no stake in the power struggle, perished.

In January 1977 the revolution guards came to our house. Girma of Arat Kilo and his gang came, one of whom was a day laborer at the mill behind our house where he fed the grain to the mills. Asrat also carried pianos and was one of the five or six who did that job for us. They ordered my grandmother and sisters to the living room. One of them with a gun slung over his shoulder watched them, as I gave Girma and the others a tour. We opened all the drawers, cupboards and refrigerators. When I opened the freezer, which revealed six raw chickens one of them asked, "what do you do with the six?" I answered, "we use them one at a time. They can remain frozen for months." Oh, the silly things you remember when revolutionaries invade your home. A good two hours had passed when they finally left, taking with them my childhood air gun. Three days later they returned; it was almost midnight, I had somehow expected them and waited to take my shower at that hour. I heard the door, and when I came out of the bathroom, they were already at the front of the door.

I saw shadows through the translucent glass on the door. I put on the robe and came out, water dripping all over me. Girma gasped looking at my hairy chest; I was bigger than him. He started asking me where the instruments were? In Amharic in the colloquial language, they use the word instrument for guns, and I deliberately directed them to the shelf where we had a saxophone alto, a saxophone soprano, a trumpet and a broken arm of a trombone. I showed them slowly one by one, Girma was irritated and asked where our father was, and I told him he is in the hospital and my mother is there with him. At about 1:00 AM they left. It was perhaps the first time that I used my non-Ethiopian origin pretending that I did not understand the Amharic slang.

The rumors in Arat Kilo was that Girma of kebele (Urban Dwellers Association) 07 is the henchman of Mengistu. What we witnessed was red blood in the streets. He regularly executed people opposite our house, just like that. No reason. No explanation.

Just bang. Gunshots. Death in the streets. I will refrain from any descriptions but for one that shall serve as the example of what we saw on any typical day in that time. A woman, in her last term of pregnancy with five others who had just finished the evening shift at Berhanena Selam Printing Press, left the building and were executed on the spot. Right there and then, in the open space opposite our house. What I saw was beyond my comprehension; these people had nothing to mark them as a suspect of having party associations or political agendas; they were just returning home after a hard night's work. What I saw was purely an exhibition of authority, power, and anarchy.

The day after the execution of the six from Berhanena Selam Printing Press the workers decided to strike. The newspaper stopped and the Girma, guardian of the revolution, was being sought by the revolution.

Troops were sent in to chase out Girma and his gang. Girma was apprehended when he tried to arrest Mengitsu's uncle. After this incident, there was an order placed to stop Girma's vigilante activity terrorizing Addis Ababa.

They finally arrested Girma and his gang. Girma was sentenced to die, and the whole neighborhood went to Shiro Meda, where the firing squad put them down. One eyewitness later told me, that Girma had tried to say something but a bullet cut his speech short.

Was it a reign of terror, or an organized slaughter, and was it initiated and supported by the Derg, and are the governing elite answerable to crimes against humanity? The answer to all is an unhesitant YES.

The revolution eats its children (Abyot lidjun yibelal). It became a favorite saying in those days.

The EPRP vanished from the scene in 1978, those who escaped the purge to the interiors joined the various liberation fronts forming under the Eritrean Liberation Front, like the TPLF the Tigrean People's Liberation Front and the Eritrean People's Liberation Front. A few remnants of the EPRP after the overthrow of the Mengistu regime came back to assume power with the EPRDF, and a few left a massive scar on the development of Ethiopia with their extreme ideas.

The MEISON taught the communist jargon to their champion Mengistu, who eliminated them from the government with no trace once he could parrot the slogans.

I was in the Ethiopian Rubber, and Canvas Shoe Factory (now sold to New Wing a Chinese company) for a sales call when I heard gunshots from the nearby factory Addis Tyre. Both were share companies established by government financing in agreement with Czechoslovakia at that time. They probably employed over three thousand workers and had powerful labor unions, which in those days imprisoned, tried and executed people. The manager coolly escorted me out, whispering that there is unrest in Addis Tyre. I started my car, and I was just out of the compound, when someone opened the rear door of my car and jumped in, he had a pistol in his hand but did not threaten me. I calmly drove, just when I crossed the railway line in front of the factory, a car from Addis Tyre flew out of the compound and started to chase me down. The Toyota pick-up had more power than mine, but it was not fast. I could not stop as they would shoot at me so pressing on the gas was the only alternative. I noticed a newly paved road on the right, towards Wollo Sefer, near the railway junction, popularly labeled as "The confusion square." I took that road and reduced my speed to accommodate the dirt road. The chasing car drove straight. After a few hundred meters I stopped the car, my legs were trembling. No questions asked and without any explanation, the fugitive thanked me and ran out. After that, I never used that car to visit those two customers. I borrowed my sister's car.

In those difficult times, there were too many guardians of the revolution who had complete authority to arrest, kill, incarcerate and judge people. These included the Kebekes, the worker's unions, the cadres in the factories, the police and security. In that chaos, many vanished without a trace. No one was safe. You just had to be lucky, not to be the one killed. Relatives were not allowed to mourn the death of their "counterrevolutionary" beloved ones, and if they asked for the body, they were forced to pay for the bullets that took the innocent life.

We had two Volkswagen pickups, and these became the target of the multifunction office with whom we shared the compound. In 1977 every Saturday we received a letter saying they needed the cars for the revolution. We could not be against the revolution, and to prove it we used to give them the vehicles. These were used and abused, and we did the repairs. With the overloading an axle, a spring or a shock-absorber would break or bend. The newer pickup we took it to the garage and sold it from there. The second one remained with us for about six months. We agreed to co-operate with the transport, provided one of us drove. At one point when driving out of the compound, their driver bumped into one of our other cars..

My mother, my sister Salpi or I used to drive them around, whether to move an orchestra or an office, but the worst was when we had to transport detainees. The one time, looking out of the window of a bedroom, I noticed three well-dressed young girls, unlike the detention of the street girls who were brought there during the curfew hours. They were called in and out several times. Finally, there was a knock on our door; it was for the car.

Salpi volunteered to drive; I said no, I would drive. I knew it had to do something with those girls. I went down opened the door, and they pushed the girls in, and two revolutionary guards followed into the car. We drove to two or three different places. In the end, we went into the compound across from Itegue Mennen school. The guardians of the revolution left the girls in the car alone with me. I questioned them. They were forced to go to an indoctrination session in their kebele and had attended the "lecture" at the end of it the lecturer had said "the revolution is above everything" raising his left arm with the closed fist, repeating it three times. All the attendants raised their hands except for these girls. Apparently, that was a counter-revolutionary action sufficient to detain them. After being kept overnight they were asked to say the slogan, but they adamantly refused. Arguing that, "Only God is above everything."

The fifteen to twenty minutes when we were alone in the car, I tried to reason with these girls telling them God will understand if you save your lives and repent later by extra prayers. They did belong to another sect and were not Ethiopian Orthodox. Finally, the guards came, and they violently pushed them into a room behind the main house. I hope God saved their lives, but I will never know.

The media that exposed the famine in Ethiopia to the world and helped the downfall of a regime somehow managed to turn deaf, dumb and blind to the atrocities of the unlawful assault on civilian life. Why did they keep silent when hundreds were perishing daily due to the violence in addition to the increasing hunger? It was an enigma to me that the United States of America, with all its presence in Ethiopia made no effort to intervene or persuade Mengistu.

Finally, the praised man of the US Media, the strongman Mengistu, attacked the US presence in Ethiopia when in 1977 he threw out the United States Information Services (USIS), the Naval American Medical Research Unit 5 (NAMRU 5), the Mapping Mission, the Kagnew Station and the Military Assistance Advisory Group (MAAG). With the expulsion of these organizations, we had to transport over twenty pianos to our house. We sold them when our father fell sick in bed. Dismantling a business was sad, but we did it then, and we were obliged to do it yet again.

Mengistu had no choice but to turn full left towards the Eastern Bloc. The USSR armed Somalia, and with substantial Soviet military presence in Somalia, Siad Barre of Somalia attacked Ethiopia even though at the same time, Siad Barre had been flirting with the West. The Somalis advanced up to Awash without significant resistance. Mengistu pledged allegiance to the Soviets, who on both sides of the war had advisors initially but chose Ethiopia in the end. The old American arsenal in Ethiopia was replaced with Soviet modern MIGs and AK47 machine guns. Ethiopia lost its gold reserve and the positive trade balance. It lost everything and started accumulating debt, under the management of inexperienced ministers running the economy. The shelves of the supermarkets emptied.

The destitution persisted.

The Red Terror continued despite the Somali attack. History has shown that during any external attack Ethiopians put aside their differences to fight the enemy, but for Mengistu concentrating on the internal conflict seemed more crucial. With the shameful defeat, Mengistu should have sought an honorable Seppuku instead of growing his rank to colonel.

The once strong Ethiopian army with its educated generals a decade back had reached the gates of Mogadishu under the command of General Michael Aman Andom. The Derg executed many of those strategists, and now the sergeants and the lieutenants were replacing them. Apart from the Ethiopian Airforce which was performing heroic acts, the Somali army advanced up to Awash. Fidel Castro with 120,000 soldiers came to Ethiopia's rescue. It was not only Cuba, but Ethiopia owes its victory to the Yemenis, East Germans and Soviets with whose assistance it pushed back the Somali army, and the war ended in March 1978. Finally, in 1991 Siad Barre, the Ethiopian born Somali, was exiled. A few years later Somalia went into a civil war.

Destruction awaits those who meddle with Ethiopia.

CHAPTER ELEVEN

Every day was a risky day, one never knew what would happen next, but we got used to that tension. After 1978 the street killings and random assassinations subsided. Mengistu's shocking defeat by the Somalis prompted him to strengthen the army, and in one of his speeches, he boasted that apart from the militia, Ethiopia had an army of a million men, the biggest in Africa. And yet he lost every battle.

As a consequence, scarcity caused people to start hoarding, and this paved the way for entrepreneurial risk-takers to accumulate wealth very rapidly. A nouveau-riche class started to form quickly; replacing the middle class. While the middle class was generally the educated elite, the nouveau-riche were streetwise. It altered the entire face of the supply industry, the ethics of distributing quality items gave way to trading the cheapest. There was a waste of already scarce foreign exchange on inferior goods. To boost the morale of high-ranking officers, government officials received new cars, with a designated driver. The government started bribing its executives, which became the norm and insidiously became part of the culture of governance.

Indeed, the morale of the nationalized factory managers was very high, and they worked conscientiously and with dedication. They had taken their assignments seriously and were learning fast. Amongst the managers, there were some who would not even accept a simple pen, which we distributed as a form of thank you and advertisement. From 1979 to 1982 business was good for a lot of people, including me. I built a reputation for reliability and efficient service. If I said I could deliver a chemical from Antwerp to Assab, it would happen with no shenanigans. Another aspect that became beneficial for the company was our ability to work discreetly, especially during emergencies. Our company supplied medication and capsules when there were outbreaks of diarrhea and nausea. Even though everyone knew what was going around was cholera, the government refrained from calling it that. They, until recently in 2019, classified it under the umbrella term "Acute Water Diarrhea." We delivered the medical supplies, quietly, efficiently and without any news breaking in the media. And Epharm (The Ethiopian Pharmaceutical Company) much appreciated us for the complete and reliable discretion with which we got things done.

We also were the approved supplier of cigarette seam adhesive and going through the purchasing system we supplied the required glue. In general, I avoided the supply of sensitive items, but on two occasions I faced severe allegations of sabotage. It was January, the time of year that nights got very cold, usually going down below zero degrees Celsius. I was summoned to the Tobacco Monopoly. An Armenian, Matig Kevorkoff established the Tobacco Monopoly in the 1920s. It was the function of this committee to look at the production waste. On that occasion I was under investigation for selling adhesive that did not hold the seams of the cigarettes together.

The paper had not closed, and on those fast running machines, which produced several thousand cigarettes per minute, the wastage was significant. The revenue authorities, supervising the production for the collection of excise tax were furious, reporting the incident to their head office. We concocted a fresh batch of the glue, cleaned the machine and by noon everything was running well. I tried to explain, but the waste from the night had made them unreceptive, so I said I would consult the chemists at the factory in Germany and come back with a reply. Later I visited the evening shift, checked the production and the machine was running well. The next morning, I went back. As soon as I entered the compound, I understood that they had faced the same problem as the previous night and this time they directed me to a different office. The room was austere red, decorated with many red flags and photos of Marx, Engels, and Lenin with the hammer and sickle threatening the onlooker. It was the room of the political cadre of the factory, and it was very intimidating. I had lived six years in the Soviet Union, so I knew the rhetoric that would follow my reception. They accused me of sabotaging the economy, and with the faulty product I was aiding the counter-revolutionaries at the north, and so on. After thirty minutes of accusations exhausting all the vocabulary of the party propaganda from the dictionary, he allowed me to speak. Luckily Henkel had checked the samples of the batches and had found no defect. We delivered, as we always did, viable, quality adhesive. It was the cold night temperature that caused a hike in the drying time thus causing the seams to open. The solution was to increase the temperature of the ironing rod or add a solvent during the evening to quicken the setting time of the glue. They chose the second option, so I borrowed the recommended glycol from another factory and saved the revolution.

The repercussions of the other encounter would have been more severe had I not been as cautious as I was with the order. It was a tender of 600 tons of newsprint paper that we had won with our bid. I later learned that the supply was to come from Romania with a transshipment involved, in the Eastern Mediterranean. This made me panic. I asked our London office to supply me two sets of pro-forma for half the quantity each, and then I went to Berhanena Selam Printing Press giving them one set for 300 tons. I suggested that they ask for a counterbid from the second winner, who was their regular supplier. The competitor jumped on the occasion, splitting the order.

There were so many obstacles and issues with completing this order that in my 35 years of experience, I had never faced as many problems on a single order as I had encountered with this one. We shipped all orders within three to four weeks but with this order, after six weeks there was still no vessel, and finally, in the seventh week, a smaller liner was found for loading. The ship left for the Eastern Mediterranean but sank when a missile hit it, with our newsprint order on it. After two whole months of trying to resolve many problems, including insurance, and document amendments, the second batch was shipped, and I was relieved that the transshipment was going to be in Jeddah and not somewhere else. The vessel arrived in Jeddah, but the newsprint paper was held there. It would take a small ship six to eight hours from Jeddah to Assab, but the vessel was not allowed to move or unload in Jeddah for reasons that I did not understand.

The customer demanded an explanation. When I got there to explain I was directed to the manager's office and guess what? He was military. After many accusations, I told him that the matter was with the Jeddah port authority and out of our control. We had no means of direct communication, so we must go through the shipping line. After a few days, they called me again, and three people in the manager's office started shouting on me. I kept my calm, and with a smile, I told them I do not know how to sail a vessel; otherwise, I would go and bring the boat to Assab. They laughed. The next day while I was going to Modjo, I saw many loaded trucks with newsprint paper, heading to Addis Ababa, a sigh of relief, the lot of the competitor had arrived. Ours arrived ten weeks later.

On March 10, 1979, our son Garen was born. On the third day after his arrival, Dr. Kevork apologized, that the hospital had just admitted many casualties and all beds were assigned to the wounded, who were flown in from the North. We left the hospital with our baby Garen and went home. There were many experienced elders at hand, my mother and grandmother, and Dr. Kevork who was a cousin. There were no complications. A few months later the pediatrician told us that Garen needed to have a minor operation, but because there were no anesthesiologists for infants, we had to take him abroad.

We put in a request at the immigration office for Mary's exit visa, but they rejected the application because Mary would not be able to take an Ethiopian child abroad with her stateless status. Again, the question of citizenship was haunting us. We applied for the citizenship, and the person in charge asked us to wait, and when we were the only ones in the room, he discreetly asked if we seriously wanted the Ethiopian Nationality, at a time when many were giving it back. After we assured him, he ordered the file and told us he could not process her nationality as she has been rejected and reversing it would take time. I asked him the reason, and he said, the report mentioned that while she can speak six languages very well, she did not speak Amharic. He asked me to change the application and apply for her as my wife, the daughter-in-law of Nerses Nalbandian. After making sure that Mary spoke Amharic, they finally granted her Ethiopian citizenship. Mary and Garen left on the flight together with our good friends Robert and Tecla, who were leaving Ethiopia for good.

In 1979 our mother and I traveled to Montreal, Canada to attend the wedding of my brother Harout to his fiancée, Seza. Despite all the difficulties, our managing to be present was a great achievement. This visit paved the way for my mother and grandmother to emigrate to Canada in 1982.

The following years we did not experience significant changes, things had calmed down, and everything fell into a welcomed routine with an active baby who vied for our attention. Garen kept us busy at home under the auspices of a dismembered community leadership that needed revival.

The younger members of the community were departing, and the elderly in most cases had nowhere to go. As the Archdeacon, I headed the church and for officiations asked the Greek or an Ethiopian priest to conduct the ceremonies. Once there was a suicide case, and according to the practices, neither the Ethiopian nor the Greek priests would do the entombment ceremony. The person was a benefactor of the community. I consulted Mr. Averdis Terzian, and we concluded that it was not up to us to judge a person who could hardly move and was bedridden for many months and had put an end to his misery. I performed the ceremony and that was the beginning of that additional duty on me — something that was emotionally taxing to do because I knew every individual who died from childhood.

I cannot say that there was appreciation, recognition or respect for what I did, but what I have seen in the eyes of the relatives of the deceased was a request for my help. My help was limited to the ceremonies, as I am not a chosen one, but I treated and served each family equally well, despite how hard it was to be the one to bury someone whom I knew for years. A person who initially criticized our church service became our greatest supporter, telling me "in the service of the community you surpassed your father".

I had to travel for training in Dusseldorf and meet my employers in London. Mary had a free ticket allowance on Alitalia, and we combined business with our first chance to travel together and called it a belated honeymoon. It was September 1980. We transited in Rome and flew to Frankfurt, where Vilma Stordiau drove from Vienna to meet up with her childhood friend Mary. We had a fabulous time with the Staurdiaus family and then left for Dusseldorf. A representative from Henkel's leather department received us at the airport. We stayed at a hotel near the shopping district, near "Koenig's Alee," where all the big fashion brands have their outlets in Dusseldorf. We visited Koln with its magnificent cathedral and climbed to the top of the bell tower. Soon after we left for London where we stayed a few days and then flew to Paris.

Edouard Badvaganian, my friend for many years both in Melkonian and Yerevan, met us at the airport, and we spent four days of sightseeing and enjoyment. Off to Rome, we flew, where we had a lengthy stopover. Krikor and Rita Boghossian took us around Rome, so we didn't have to sit around at the airport with nothing to do. After a memorable dinner with Rita's mother, we left to the airport to catch our flight to Los Angeles. Mary's brother Benon and his wife Sandy met us at the airport, and we had an unforgettable time visiting the extravaganza of the film industry. We met a few relatives specifically Mary's aunt, Vartuhi and her husband, Yervant Derentz and their children. Our effort to meet other relatives of Mary proved impossible as the husband of a cousin of Mary said, they didn't have time for us. Years later he needed my help when his brother passed away, and I reminded him of his words but, because I have integrity,

I did not deny him the help he needed. Unlike him, I was a leader in the community. Instead Armen and Salpi Kerassimian hosted us for two nights, and we enjoyed the anecdotes of our memories of the year we shared in room 76 in the hostel in Yerevan. They took us to Los Angeles airport to fly to Montreal via Chicago O'Hare airport.

Harout, Seza and their first born, Tamar received us at the airport and brought us to their house. Some ex-Ethio Armenians came to see us curious to hear about the happenings in Ethiopia. However, no one dared ask the obvious question, "were they right in their decision to leave Ethiopia." It was astonishing for many to see a husband and wife traveling together from the terror-stricken dictatorship, which they had left in a rush. Yet here a couple had crossed half the globe to visit relatives. We visited the tourist sites of Montreal and its surrounding area. It was time to go back to our lives in Ethiopia.

Soon after our return to Addis Ababa a conscientious bank manager came to church on a Sunday and informed me of abuse taking place on the bank accounts of an old lady who lived alone. It began with people who started to help her to the bank. At first, there were frequent small withdrawals that grew over time to more substantial amounts. I asked my mother to visit the old lady to see what was going on. People were taking advantage of Mrs. Anna Terzian, who upon being asked, agreed to give her bank saving books to the young priest, and that was me. We got the books, and when she fainted in church, we reopened a new account where we deposited all her money from the 12 branches in this single account with two signatories, Mr. Edward Kevorkian and myself. We appointed Mrs. Mary Sarkissian, the caretaker of our church, to supervise Mrs. Anna against a monthly fee. The arrangement worked out very well, and the scamming stopped.

On the 8th of April, 1982, Mrs. Anna passed away; we made all the necessary arrangements for her funeral and informed her sister, to whom she wished to pass all her earthly belongings. Mrs. Rebecca Der Boghossian thanked me for telling her and asked me to call her after the burial. We talked to her and tried to convince her to come to Ethiopia, but she said she was not interested in anything the sister had acquired by living in misery and suggested that I do whatever I wanted to do with the money. I asked her to give me the contact details of her daughter, and she did, but I had to cut our conversation as we had to take Mary to the hospital to give birth. Despite Mary's pleas to the Czech doctor to be around as she felt she was going to have the baby the next day, the doctor had gone sightseeing. We had to look for a doctor as we were expecting complications. Mary Messrobian put us in touch with Dr. Robert Markaryan from Soviet Armenia. We rushed to the hospital before the curfew, and the doctor came at which point we immediately began to explain the predicted complications, but Dr. Robert dismissed it. At one point, Dr. Robert came to me and said - your wife does not understand Armenian come in to translate to her. That was a misunderstanding created because of the Eastern and Western Armenian dialects. At 5:00 am Mary had Elise and Dr. Robert told me to take them home because once again, as was the case with Garen, the hospital beds were needed for the many admissions of wounded soldiers. We left the hospital as soon as the paperwork was finalized.

We were witness to the cost of human life for the second time visiting the hospitals twice in three years; we saw the continuous loss of innocent lives. Something that can be avoided by simple dialogue and ceding positions by both warring sides will always be a better solution than sacrificing the lives of citizens. But the greed of the leaders and weapon suppliers is never satiated.

Coming back to the inheritance of Mrs. Anna Terzian, after we explained to her daughter Anna about the aunt's death and circumstances, Mrs. Rebecca agreed to spend a few days in Ethiopia. We sent her a first-class ticket and booked her into the Ethiopia Hotel as she had made it very clear that she would not want to see her sister's house. She took a substantial sum for herself, paid the schooling and ticket of a student to Melkonian and made a generous gift to my daughter Elise. The rest she gave to me to use as I found fit. The collapsed external wall of the cemetery was my priority in those days, and after the completion of that, the wooden fence of the club, which collapsed every rainy season, that I upgraded next. On the wall of the cemetery, a marble stone marks "built by the donation of Mrs. Rebecca Der Boghossian."

Two months after Elise was born, my mother and grandmother emigrated to Canada. At the end of October after a business trip to Dusseldorf and London, I went to Canada to see how they were doing. There were actions to be taken.

CHAPTER TWELVE

On September 13, 1983, members of the Ethiopian Control Committee arrested all of the Armenian staff of Hagbes, a leading hardware store in Addis Ababa belonging to our cousin, including my younger sister Salpi and our cousin Hrair. The accusation was the usual, "economic sabotage". Everyone was released almost immediately except for Salpi who was let go a few days later, on Friday. While all this was going on, I was in Canada with my family, and we didn't hear about the arrest until we arrived in London. My managers, Vartan and Jirayr informed me about it with a gloomy face and even invited me to prolong my stay in London until everything was worked out. It was out of the question for me.

On Monday the 12th of December 1983, Salpi went to her job in Hagbes, and when she came home for lunch, she was restless, uneasy looking out of the front window into the parking lot of the Control Committee. The accountant was behaving strangely, making threats, and she had an eerie feeling something was coming. The Hagbes' accountant was a good friend of the director of of the Ethiopian Control Committee.

The Committee offices were situated across our house in the confiscated Emanuel Baptist Church building, where the church hall was divided into cubicles and converted to interrogation rooms. Salpi did not have to wait long. The SUVs moved and headed directly over to our house. Armed people controlled the gate and others ran up the stairs and forcefully shoved the door open, entering the corridor where my little boy Garen of only four years and seven months old was innocently playing on the floor with some toys. They kicked the toys aside and demanded to see Salpi. Two of them grabbed her arms and dragged her out of the house as if she was resisting which she was not. Seeing the weapons and how roughly they treated his aunt, Garen automatically responded by attacking them. They were ready to hit the baby Garen as well, but we calmed him down and took him to the kitchen.

We went down and asked where they were taking her to no avail. Going out of the compound they said - we will let you know where to bring her food. Their efforts to control Hagbes failed and they blamed Salpi, because of Salpi's presence, so they decided to eliminate her.

After four hours of waiting alone worrying about her fate, they finally took her to the first police station in Sidist Kilo. A jail in ruins, with woodlouse racing down from the ceiling to the floor, the observer would see the mahogany wall vibrating with their movement; we delivered insecticide to calm the race of the bugs. The next day, we provided Baygon concentrate to disinfect the room. We replaced the blanket and the mattress the second day after the disinfection and burned the first ones.

A few days later they transferred her to the third police station (not the security prison), which underwent the same disinfection process and finally, they moved her to the second police station. They didn't inform us of the transfer; it was top secret. We kept asking the guards at the police station, and even though they knew very well that she was no longer there, they enjoyed keeping us outside waiting to deliver the food to her.

After about a ½ hour we were able to ask the chief of the police station for information. Oh, how they all loved to watch us squirm. In his position, the chief would build on our anxiety, slowly opening the logbook, making a few phone calls, until finally asking a subordinate to bring Salpi's file to him. All this slow motion to finally get to the point. Salpi wasn't even there. Police brutality is a common phenomenon with different degrees of manifestation in different countries, and thankfully, Salpi was not treated with cruelty like the other inmates, as she was a "guest" of the police station and not one of theirs.

The principal felons in the police station were prostitutes, curfew offenders, and bar attendants involved in fights. There were also female pickpockets. Their specialty was to empty pockets in busses. How they did this was; the bus driver would break very suddenly, throwing people off balance and the pickpockets would "wrap themselves to a target," taking what they could and then thanking the victim for saving them from falling. It gave the unsuspecting victims the satisfaction of helping an attractive young girl. At day's end shared the profits with the driver.

Two of these girls were regulars at the police station where Salpi was being held. They protected her when a mentally ill person would come late at night into the cell after curfew hours and attack Salpi. When this happened, these two girls would karate kick Salpi's attacker and put her at an opposite corner and order her not to move. The second police station was a 3-minute walk from our house which made it less of a strain for Mary to go. Of course, the whole neighborhood knew where Mary was going and always asked how Salpi was doing.

After five months Salpi was transferred to the Central Intelligence Bureau, the notorious "Mehakelawi" prison. This was much more of a strain on Mary, with a completely new routine for logistics and food preparation, and another adjustment for Salpi to a new environment that was populated with educated and highly placed people instead of pickpockets and prostitutes.

Just before Salpi's transfer to "Mehakelawi," the two girls spent another week in prison, this time for stealing a necklace belonging to one of the girls' mother's and then selling the stolen item. The mother had the girls arrested, but these girls were super, they knew how to play the game. Under interrogation, one denied stealing, and neither of them would reveal the whereabouts of the necklace. Without answers or evidence, and within the two day limitation, the police took them to court. The girls denied the charges, even though they had admitted to the crime in the police station. They both declared that they admitted guilt in the police station under duress. The court granted extra time, the police strengthened his interrogation technics, and one of the girls agreed to show where she sold the necklace. Needing a female attendant to go with the girl but unable to find one, the interrogator volunteered to take the girl to show him the jewelry. Flirtatious and manipulative, the girl directs him out of town to Sululta and shows him a good time instead of leading him to the stolen necklace. They returned late in the evening, and the next day the court had no choice but to release them for lack of evidence. These young girls late in their teens knew all the loopholes of the law for their crimes.

Meanwhile, over in "Mehakelawi," they took Salpi into a crowded room. Salpi started to make a mental estimate of how she could place her mattress in that room. One girl approached her, took the bed from Salpi's arms and placed it next to hers whispering authoritatively in French, "do not trust anyone; they are all involuntary informers." The girl was Haimanot Gebreegziabeher a political prisoner, who had done translations for her uncles who plotted a coup against Mengistu. She was in prison for already over two years and had seniority in the room. Salpi and Haimi became good friends, and she remained a good friend to the whole family until she passed away.

Amongst the others in the room, there was Mengistu's secretary a beautiful girl, the lover of a high-ranking person, and Mengistu's chief of protocol a highly educated girl from Sorbonne. Their crime? It was being Tigrean. Mengistu, who was losing the war against the joint forces of the Eritrean and Tigrean liberation fronts, cracked down on all Tigreans and imprisoned and tortured them. During interrogation, an abused victim giving in agreed to have recruited the whole list presented to her. That meant new prisoners in the rooms. At one point there were twenty-three prisoners in a cell that could barely accommodate ten. There was a system devised for sleeping with minimum space use, heads to toes and toes to heads. There were a couple of informants also placed amongst the prisoners, who gathered information and passed it to the torturers. These informants even pretended that they were coming back from the torture room.

Salpi was a guest to the "Mehakelawi," so she was free from any interrogation or torture, and they did not bother her. There was, however, one time when they brought in one of the girls who was a regular for punishment. One of the favorite torturing methods used in prison was to fix a piece of wood behind the knees, tie the legs tightly and suspend the body upside down then hit the behind and under the feet with a lash. They brought this poor girl in, beaten under the feet and bruised on her bum. She could not sit or stand up. Salpi treated her wounds (for which she was severely reprimanded but mercifully not physically punished). Those tortured in this way could not walk for many days, nor sit without a great deal of pain. Salpi and Haimi studied the pattern of this particular girl's interrogation days, which always came after the day she confided to the informant. Salpi got a warning after advising this girl not to divulge to the informant.

Mary took food every day at 11:00 and delivered it through the window, after tasting the food. The sampling of the food was to prevent poisoning and was practiced everywhere in the jails and prison. "Mamish" the godmother of our cousin, despite our insistence to the contrary, insisted on looking after her godson, and for two and a half years she did so very well. After she was taken ill, Mary took over that duty as well. Our family got a reprimand from an old Armenian lady; it was not her place to do it, allowing "Mamish" to deliver the food to Hrair, who was at the time alone in Ethiopia. We tried to see both Salpi and Hrair, but the permission had to come from the Control Committee, and it did not come. After eight months of trial, we finally succeeded in seeing Salpi, and that was with the help of Archbishop Zaven Chinchinian, who asked to see the prisoners. They could not refuse him. It happened that the commander of "Mehakelawi" was a graduate from Cairo, from where the Archbishop came. They chatted for a few minutes, and that broke the ice. The commander told the Archbishop in Arabic that he would allow our visitations.

During Holy Week, Mary prepared traditional Easter bread and colored eggs and brought the children with her to visit Salpi. Parking the car outside, she guided Garen and Elise into the compound. A car came in, passed them and then backed-up and asked in English, "Madame, do you know where you are?" And Mary replied, "sure, I brought the children to see their aunt before Easter." The official asking was Fesseha Desta the third person in command, and when I arrived a moment later to join my family, I managed to joke, "Sure we know where we're going! We're taking a stroll through Central Park." The commander left us alone in his office, and we stayed over an hour catching up with Salpi on every detail. Salpi used to go through books by the dozen a week, and there were none to buy in town, but thanks to some diplomat friend we brought reading material. The delivery of reading material was through another window and went straight to censorship. There was a Harlequin Romance book by Amanda Carpenter titled "The Great Escape." After a day of handing in this book, they asked Mary to go to the office, and the person in charge, scolded – are you implying something with this book? The explanation of the title was on the back cover if he read it. The paranoia of the officers in "Mehakelawi" was to the maximum. They were suspicious of everything and everyone and were arrogant and brutal. Whether it was part of their training or nature, I could not tell. Twenty years later, when "Mehakelawi" arrested Arsho for testing HIV, I concluded that the paranoia came with the profession.

    The Derg celebrated its tenth anniversary with pomp and extravaganza. In 1985 Mengistu visited Pyongyang from where he took inspiration and brought experts to prepare for the parades. The government lavished Addis Ababa with unnecessary monuments, metallic arches, banners, decorations, and trained thousands of youngsters for the show on Revolution Square. What was Mengistu celebrating? A shameful lost war against Somalia, losing battles in the north against EPLF and TPLF, a complete economic catastrophe, or the ever-increasing famine; it was incomprehensible. On top of the disasters, he forced all government employees to wear the dark blue, light blue, and khaki uniforms, while he wore an elegant outfits with high collars tailored by high-fashion designers. It was something extraordinary.

Mengistu's extravagant "uniform" triggered quotes from George Orwell's "Animal Farm." "All animals are equal, but some are more equal than the others."

In consequence of this extravaganza, the economy collapsed, and the government banned driving on Sundays while giving seven-liter petrol coupons that worked only on the weekends. Mengistu also repossessed the cars from the government managers which were provided to them generously by the regime, after which I noticed the change in the attitude of the managers and the consequent failure of the factories. The wars, the inexperience, and the egotistical megalomania of Mengistu brought the country to a grinding halt. Ethiopia was a failed state.

One day Mary called me to rush home. When I reached the house I saw Mary talking to someone in the compound. We went in and the person informed us that the Central Control Committee has started interrogating Herair. She also informed us that they were making him sign letters to his business contacts in Europe the content of which she did not know. I was going to England a few days later for the business so I thought to contact his agents in Germany. However, when I called them to inform about the latest development, I got a rude reception saying that I should not involve them in this matter. I apologized and put down the telephone receiver. I contacted my aunt and informed her the general situation. She told me her elder son Eddie was in London. We met and I explained to him and together visited some relative and he departed.

Every Tuesday afternoon the public prosecutor of the special court received relatives who had a pending court case. Mary and I were regular visitors to the office of the deputy head of the prosecutor of the special court. Week after week his reply was the same – it is a complicated case, and we are working on it. Girma Waqjira, who probably felt like the almighty sitting in his big chair, finished our two to three hours waiting in a few seconds. One day, when he finished his sentence, I took out my pen from my pocket and said, "We have a problem. If someone told you this is an airplane, even though you know what you see is the pen, you believe it's an airplane. Start the court case, and you will realize that I am right". He blew his top and told us from now on only your wife can have the privilege, you cannot come. I burst out saying if you are man enough I will see you in court. Mary did not go to see him for a couple of weeks and then she went. She gathered up her courage and went in. That day the head of the prosecutors received her and Mary said what we rehearsed at home. "There is a rumor around town that you are taking bribes to delay the investigation as you don't have enough of a case to take it to court." Mezgebu jumped out of his chair, called the investigators and said – I want this case in court within a week. In two weeks the court case started.

We went to the palace where the special court was, with separate lawyers for Salpi and Herair. The doors opened, and we took our positions as directed and waited for the judge to come. Girma put on his cloak and took his corner. Our glances met. I had a smile after four years; finally, there was a party to listen to our version of the story. Three judges came in, everyone in the courtroom stood up until they made themselves comfortable in their chairs. The central judge looked at the file in front of him and asked if if everyone had the accusations; our lawyers said they do not have them and the usher handed over the copies. They postponed it to the afternoon. We studied the case during that brief period. One of the accusations was undeclared sales (concealing sales from the accountant by hiding invoice pads). They had some pads as evidence, and Salpi showed the lawyer the signature of the accountant on every page. Herair's lawyer, who had difficulty in understanding, got the point and when we went in, after the guilty or not guilty question, the answer for which was "not guilty", the prosecutor, with confidence started explaining his case, emphasizing the concealed invoices. Herair's lawyer objected and started pointing out the signature of the accountant on every page. The judges said to proceed, but the lawyer adamantly continued until recess. We got time to study the cases. After four years without any questions asked, the case against Salpi was "economic sabotage" for 250 U.S. Dollars and 70 UK pounds found in our safe, and an accomplice to Herair.

"I Want to Die with a Flag"

I studied Herair's case the whole night and prepared a resumé for the lawyers indicating the weaknesses of the evidence. The session the next day was exciting as our lawyers crushed the case of the prosecutor. I omit details, but at one point the prosecutor again brought up the hidden pads. The court allowed Herair and Salpi to go to the office to collect their evidence. During the next session, the prosecutor called his principal witness, the accountant. We had a truckful of files and pads brought to the court and Gebrehiwot, Herair's lawyer started the cross-examination. He took out the pads one by one and asked the accountant if the signature is his or not. He continued for three consecutive days until the accountant started crying. The judges tried to stop Gebrehiwot several times, but to no avail, he insisted that he must prove that there was no concealed invoice. Finally, the judge said you made your point, now proceed. Abebe Worke, Salpi's lawyer, presented the second key of the safe as evidence to prove that the safe did not belong to Salpi alone. With this, an acquittal for Salpi was imminent, but the acquittal did not happen as the second accusation against Salpi was as an accomplice to Herair, giving Abebe also the chance to cross-examine the witnesses, ultimately strengthening Herair's defense.

During the first session, the court ordered the transfer of the prisoners to the Central Prison near the O.A.U. headquarters, some twelve kilometers away from our house at a heavily congested area. We visited the prison on our Sunday afternoons, even with the restriction of no cars on the road on Sundays and spent some time with Salpi and Herair across a double fence. During one such visit, Yeghia Chorbadjian came with us, and while visiting Herair, my uncle introduced Belay Negga standing next to Herair to Yeghia saying 'he sent me to prison for four years' and Yeghia with humor joked, 'well you cannot help it if the earth rotates.'

The case dragged on and on. Meanwhile, in September 1987 Mengistu changed his clothes and became the first president of Ethiopia. The new constitution abolished the special court and the case transferred to the high court. By the legislation, the special court did not allow bail, and with its abolishment, we applied for their release and finally, succeeded to bring Salpi home on bail on the 29th of December 1987 four years and seventeen days later. The one regret I have is that I was not in Ethiopia on the day the Public Prosecutor Girma Waqjira acknowledged that they did not have the details and withdrew the case against Herair and Salpi. A few weeks later I saw him at a cocktail event. He tried avoiding me, but I approached, took out my pen from my pocket, looked in his eyes and said, "I told you so." The government ruined the most productive years of our lives, stole years from us, with no compensation for a wrongful trial and abuse of authority.

Some years later Herair was again prosecuted. I went to some of the trials but at this time the legal system was different, and he lost the case. It was sad to see Herair alone this time.

This dreadful experience taught me one thing: There are people, who would rather evade the truth and not feel any obligation even to say a simple thank you. They ignore the persons who helped them and reward those who blamed them; it seems it is part of the nature of ungrateful people.

CHAPTER THIRTEEN

The day our father died we lost our patriarch, and the Saint Kevork Armenian church of Addis Ababa lost its pillar. To keep his legacy alive, we, his children, Hermine, Salpi and I resolved to keep it open. It was not an easy decision nor was it an easy undertaking. We were faced with a lot of controversy and resistance. The community was highly critical even though they very much wanted a well-functioning church. The Armenian clergy did not like the semi-independent status of our church. The communist state looked on from afar and questioned my legality to the extent of calling me to the patriarchate to clarify matters. An inquest was called, for which a worried Avedis Terezian accompanied me. It lasted only a few minutes.

The patriarch Abune Teklehaimanot invited us to a room where a few archbishops and a priest were present and asked me directly:

- My son, what is your education?
- I said - I am an electromechanical engineer.
- What is your background and how are you running a church?
- I replied - It is a God-given gift.

A true clergy, a person from a monastery, praying and praising God all his life, the Patriarch liked my answer, and he said:

- My son, continue with your dedicated work.

Since that day I receive invitations to all the official functions of the church, placing me alongside the other heads of different churches. My title on the envelope is Archdeacon, which I certainly am, but for few occasions, they have even referred me as Archbishop, which I am not, but I understand the reason for the "mistake," and always act accordingly.

The priest who was present at the questioning started bringing groups from the Soviet Union and describing our church to them in fluent Russian.

The first thing Armenians in the diaspora do is establish a school and build a church. Initially, the community had a humble hut serving as the church Sourp Asdvadzadzin (Mother of God) in the present club compound. The first pastor of the church was Father Hovhannes Guevherian from 1923 to 1958. However, for a brief period in 1925 Reverend Hovsep Garabedian also served as pastor. Mihran Mouradian, a wealthy investor from Istanbul, with businesses in New York and Bucharest, promised to build us a better a church should his company succeed in Ethiopia. It did, and he followed through on his promise. He bought the land of the church from the community, inherited from Krikor Hovian, and using his expenses he built the church and donated it to the Armenian Community of Ethiopia, and he invited Archbishop Kevork Arslanian to place the foundation stone of the church. In 1928 the foundation stone was set, and the church was in full swing starting 1934. The only wish Mihran Mouradian had was to name the church Saint Kevork in memory of his father. At the occasion of the placement of the foundation of the Saint Kevork church in Addis Ababa, Archbishop Kevork Arslanian was instrumental in the construction of the Saint Minas chapel in Dire Dawa, made by the donation of mainly the Minassian family in collaboration with Onnig Shahvekil and Hovhannes Varjabedian.

In 1912 Ovsanna Djerrahian initiated a study of Armenian language from her home, a few years later Araradian was established and soon after the Sanassarian school opened its doors to Armenian students. The two separate schools had different ideological inclinations based on the political parties the leaders belonged to. After the commencement of the construction of the churches, community leaders approached Matig Kevorkoff, a wealthy businessman and the owner of the tobacco monopoly, to build a school. The two schools merged and the Matig Kevorkoff school integrated all the students under one roof. The school opened its doors in 1934 and less than one year later in 1936, the Italian Fascist regime took over the building, and it was converted to an Italian school where the Armenian students remained and continued their education in Italian.

In 1943 the reinstated Ethiopian government returned the school to the Armenian community, which continued to function in the Kevorkoff building until 1984 when an illegal two-line notice from the Administration of Rented houses threw the Armenian School out from its building within 48 hours forcefully by a military squad.

Mengistu's 10th anniversary program also initiated the removal of the Jubilee Palace school so they could extend the park of the Ghion Hotel. The privatization agency acknowledged the ownership and ordered the return of the school, but then the Minister of Education, using family connections, managed to reverse the decision with another illegal letter signed by an unauthorized signatory, out of the jurisdiction of the Privatization Agency confiscating the building.

The Fascist regime maintained the Armenian students, but the Derg threw the students out, and, of course, the EPRDF rubber stamped the illegal decision. Various appeals remain unanswered still to this day. I put some blame on the president of the Federal Republic of Germany, Professor Doctor Horst Koller, who sheepishly accepted the confiscation of the original German school and provided millions of Euros of German taxpayers money to build another school, thus unconsciously encouraging the illegal occupation of community properties. When I pushed hard with the Privatization Agency, the officer told me – Why don't you forget it like the Germans and build a new school. I said, "even if I had taxpayer money I would not construct a new school but upgrade our historical one."

In the early 1980s, the Ararat Club compound and building became the playground of the youth of the Urban Dwellers Association of the neighborhood and the abuse, and the destruction was beyond imagination. Teshome Deresse, the administrator of the club, came to my office and told me, do something about the club. I was not on the board of the club and of the last seven members only two elected board members were in Ethiopia. Above all else, during the elections, my candidacy was rejected as I had just returned from my studies reasoning that I was not a member of the club yet. I met with Manoug Kuyumdjian who was on the board and told him about Teshome's request. He didn't volunteer to confront the authorities, but I persisted and said that I would go with him. In the chairman's office, they pushed me forward to speak, and I bluntly asked the chairman of the association to order the "kebele" to vacate our club. It was surprising to get a letter from the chairman that restricted them from further using the club for their entertainment.

After the completion of the club wall, I had four broken chairs repaired and called a general assembly in the club. I showed the chairs and explained the requirements to renovate the club and the chairs. Unexpectedly, Salpi donated 3,000.00 Birr, and other people in business followed her. During that evening the collection surpassed the sum required for the renovations. I called on volunteers to reorganize and reactivate the club, and a group of nine persons took charge of the challenging job.

Removing the basketball boards and extending the length of the court was the first task the volunteers undertook, converting it into a tennis court. The tennis court, the repaired chairs, and tables woke up an otherwise depressed community. Tennis, dart, and table tennis tournaments, friendly matches against other clubs and the diplomatic corps created a new atmosphere where people gathered in lighthearted and relaxed moods. The dormant club was alive again revitalized, and people came. It was a most satisfying achievement bringing with it a renewed vitality to an awakening of the community. However, the enthusiasm subsided when the community received the letter to vacate the school within two days in April 1985.

The club volunteers offered their readiness for the task, and we met at the school, the letter mentioned only the building, but when they saw the setup, in the end, it was not the school building the government wanted, but all the school desks and books including the vast library of the school. I still find and buy books from the school library on the streets of Addis Ababa. They allowed us only seven desks and Armenian books. Legesse Asfaw, the third man in command of the country along with a truckful of soldiers, were at the entrance of the school, and they pushed us out as if it was their property and we the illegal tenants. Even four decades later and to this day, when I think of the unfair treatment of the Armenian Community School, I pity the pettiness of a vast country that crushes so much of what we work hard to build. Our appeals for the continuation of our school resulted in the authorities giving us a small two-room household, ironically the only house of an Armenian adjacent to the club — the whole property given to us fit in two rooms of our school building. And, oh the irony; the Ministry of Education harasses us every year that our classrooms are not suited for teaching.

The illegal confiscation of our school caused a mess for the community. Every year we explain to the Ministry of Education that, we can't fulfill the prerequisites because they took our building and abused it to the maximum. They illegally built a new building, in the wrong place, without a proper study of the area. Finally, abandoning our building they rented it out to another school, and we suffer the consequences of all these unjustified actions. Every time we send an appeal to the Prime Minister's Office, I must ask myself the Prime Minister even bothers to read them or if the letter ever reaches his desk.

A government acts unilaterally against a small community that was the backbone of Addis Ababa and showed their power by making it hard for us. It's really unfortunate because without their interference we were such a strong group of dedicated and heartfelt people. With only one week of interruption, we reopened the school and grew it to one of the most reasonably priced, sought-after primary schools in Addis Ababa, which is open to all, for how long, it is difficult to guess.

The Saint Kevork church cannot afford a pastor, with the two trials, the funds of the community savings depleted. I, as the deacon and my family with their knowledge of the church services, take it as our moral duty to conduct the ceremonies. The fraction of the rent that the Administration of the Rented Houses gives to the community which barely covers the administrative costs of the church means that whenever necessary the school subsidizes the church expenses. Another sad story of the pettiness of the "derg" regime, which continues to this day. The proclamation is nationalizing the "extra" houses of individuals to become the property of the people; what about properties that belong to a group of people? Logically, properties belonging to communities are not "extra" houses as they do not belong to an individual.

On the other hand, according to the legislation, the Administration of Rented Houses was the organization with the authority to collect rent in Ethiopia. To solve the anomaly the Administration of Rented Houses took control of the building and every month paid 70% of the collection to the community, which amounted to Birr 5,280.00 at the time. For the past forty-three years, this was the amount that we got every month. The rents increased, but they did not honor the initial agreement. And when the regime changed the Ethiopian Orthodox Church, the Emanuel Baptist Church, The Evangelical Church, The Anwar Mosque received their properties, but the Armenian Community building, built to cover the expenses of the church, remains unreturned. The rented houses administration presented a list of buildings to the Prime Minister, which included our four stories high edifice amongst the ones that belonged to the above mentioned organisations. The others got their buildings and so far there is no decision regarding the Armenian community property.

Do the builders of Addis Ababa deserve this segregation? I do not think so. After all it was the Armenians with great diligence who initiated the crafts of the shoe, jewelry and carpet making, embroidery and tailoring. The Armenians initiated printing and paper converting, tanning, milling, blacksmith, gunsmith and tinsmith, skills, carpentry, international trade, construction, music, and photography. It was the Armenians who introduced pharmacies, watch repair and eyeglass making. Yes, Ethiopia became our motherland with the grace of its people and rulers, but the Armenians participated in placing their new country on the world map in a positive way.

In the late 1920s, Armenian parents sent their children for further studies to France and the Armenian secondary boarding school Murad-Raphael in Venice Italy. Besides their knowledge, they brought with them football culture, and with the Italian occupation, an Armenian team participated in tournaments. After the liberation of Ethiopia, the British also encouraged football, and the concept of an Addis Ababa championship was established. The Armenians had a group of good players like the Keorhadjian brothers, Purzetian, Sapsizian and others. The necessity of a club became evident, and the Ararat Sporting Association was formed in 1945, which participated in the Addis Ababa Club's championship, with a good outcome. Once the military teams took part in the tournaments and violence dominated over skills, Ararat pulled out of the competitions. Ararat continued having football teams, but they restricted themselves to games within the international and diplomatic community. When the club was built it had two tennis courts, and for a while, tennis became the favorite sport for Armenian youth. Besides the club, Samuel Behesnilian, Vahan Pogharian, and Elias Djerrahian had tennis facilities in their compounds. In the late 1950s, the club wall gave way to the widened road, and the width of the area could no longer accommodate the length of a tennis court which had North-South preferred direction for tennis. So, then the basketball court replaced the tennis courts, and it gained popularity with the Armenian youth over the other activities. Both female and male excellent teams competed up until the depletion of the Armenian Community. The very intense competition was between the Greek Community Olympiakos and the Armenian Community Ararat Club, to the extent that the Greeks brought in from Greece a professional basketball player and the Armenian's answer to that was the adoption of an American College Championship player working with the Peace Corps in Ethiopia.

The confiscation of the Kevorkoff School building stopped the club activities as the club provided the necessary space for the continuation of the school. The volunteer committee continued the dedicated work and even reached an agreement with David Garabedian to redecorate the ground floor and initiate a restaurant successfully managed by Vahan Djerrahian after his Uncle Robert abandoned serving food. During a meeting held involving the volunteers and the members of the Community Council, Mr. Berj Garabedian asked about some issues about the responsibility of the restaurant, at which point Vahan pulled back out of the club. Finally, after the fall of the Derg regime, the restaurant reopened by the sacrifice of volunteers and became a favorite dining place for the international community.

Our fight to keep the school against all the obstacles was based on the belief that we had a responsibility to maintain the legacy of all the institutions inherited from our forefathers. We dedicated ourselves out of respect for all they have done before us and acted as temporary custodians. Our duty is keeping the institutions open and create awareness in Ethiopians about the contributions of the Armenians in Ethiopia shared through the historical ties the two nations have had for centuries. It is easy to close an institution and make it less stressful for the volunteers who dedicate their time for the survival and improvement of the community. Monetary gains of the institutions should not become the primary objective. The existence and continuity of each institution can only guarantee the acceptance and the acknowledgment of the contribution of the Armenians in Ethiopia. Otherwise, the future awaiting will be similar to the Armenian communities in Asia and the deterioration of Armenian Associations today all over the world.

Elias Djerrahian, the president-elect of the community council, started wrapping his luggage to join his children in Canada, Berj Garabedian similarly to England leaving Avedis Terzian alone, who was already in his nineties. I shared my concerns with them and decided to invite Archbishop Zaven Chinchinian to visit and help us find a solution to this problem. After lengthy discussions, we agreed to appoint a representative from the club committee, another one from the school and subsequently the church. As the oldest elected member of the club committee, the Archbishop accepted my nominating Garo Tilbian. As the administrator of the school, my nominating Arakel Sakadjian found acceptance, and from the church, it was I. The appointments caused some hurt feelings among the other volunteer members. They didn't understand the strategy behind the nominations; this was a transitional period for the reorganization of the community under the umbrella of an organized group as The Armenian Community Council. Shortly after the appointment of the auxiliary members to assist Avedis Terzian, he left for a long vacation to Canada, where his son lived. For the first time, we became aware of the situation of the management and finances of the community. Rumors circulated in town to stopping these, I clarified the position in the church and invited concerned individuals to a meeting. At the meeting, it was decided that Avedis Terzian would be approached for clarifications.

Upon Avedis Terzian's return, I called a meeting, and after the clarification, we agreed to form the provisional council to get the official acknowledgment from the government under the laws of associations in Ethiopia. The change of the government brought about the restoration of the law for the associations after lengthy negotiations, The Ministry of Justice approved a new bylaw based on our historical ones, and we called an election. However, during the waiting period, the provisional council split up into two. One group without realizing the consequences believed that we should put our community under the auspices of the AGBU (Armenian General Benevolent Union). Contrarily, the core group believed in the independence of the Ethiopian Armenian Community Council under its leadership. The AGBU group even tried a hostile takeover by a court ruling, but a legally binding election preceded the final judgment, and the newly elected council started active participation for the development of the community.

However, the enthusiasm died down before the end of five years in office. There are always individuals who seek attention, and for the sake of becoming interesting, they share information from closed meetings and are rewarded with the extra attention they seek. Furthermore, I suffice to say, the clandestine analysis of the agendas outside the meetings is more valuable than participation during the discussions. I spent a lot of time preparing a bilingual agenda meeting report to keep the inexperienced members interested in the details, to impart my experience and knowledge to newer members when there was a complaint of the limitations of their command in Armenian. This attention to detail was misinterpreted as my way of "showing off my supremacy." While I was in Europe for a business trip, they created sub-committees in which I had no designated role, even in the church. I overlooked the deliberate action and did not comment on it. I asked the committees to present a description of the tasks and duties, which never happened. And finally, they delivered carefully drafted resignation letters. However, the unwritten reason for quitting was that it was impossible to work with me. I am still sorry that they left because independent participants, who are not related to the other members are essential for the unemotional balance of control over community matters.

On the 3rd of December 1993, The Republic of Armenia established Diplomatic Relations with Ethiopia. His Excellency Edward Nalbandian, who was the Ambassador of the Republic of Armenia to Egypt at the time, brought the official documentation. The community council assigned Mr. Vahak Karibian to accompany the ambassador to the office of the president of the Transitional Government of Ethiopia, His Excellency Ato Meles Zenawi.

The first ambassador to present his credentials in Ethiopia was His Excellency Sergey Manassarian. It was in December 2000 to His Excellency Dr. Negasso Gidada, the president of the Federal Democratic Republic of Ethiopia at the time, accompanied by the Consul, Fadeh Charchoghlian and me. In March 2011 Dr. Armen Melkonian presented his credentials to the then president of Ethiopia to His Excellency Girma Wolde-Giorgis accompanied by me. In October 2003 the community council marked its 100th anniversary as a council. On this occasion, the board organized a concert at the Russian Embassy Concert Hall and a reception at the Addis Ababa Hilton. The Komitas String Quartet, Edward Tatevosyan, Souren Hakhnazaryan, Alexander Kosemyan, and Aram Talalyan, gave an outstanding performance that was the talk of the town for many months. His Holiness Abune Paulos was among the diplomats and dignitaries present. His Excellency Sergey Manassarina made the introduction, followed by my speech about the occasion.

The Armenian Embassy in Egypt appreciated the services I rendered to them and established friendly relations with me even suggesting to the Ministry of Foreign Affairs of Armenia that they appoint me as the honorary consul of Armenia in Ethiopia. The Ministry approved my candidacy and proposed my appointment to the Ministry of Foreign Affairs of Ethiopia. I entrusted this information to only two people outside my immediate family and to my dismay the news leaked. The AGBU group appealed to the Ministry of Foreign Affairs mentioning that there was a court case pending against me and the Ministry asked for clarification. I cleared the accusation against me about the court case, which did not have my name mentioned at all and shamefully it was against the community. I said to the officer, it is an honor for me to be the community, but the word shows a group, not an individual. At that point, I decided not to pursue the appointment which would have meant unnecessary tension within Ethiopian Armenians and additional expenses that come with the position. I told the officer I would not sacrifice the community for recognition.

On the 18th of October 2000, His Holiness Karekin II the Catholicos of all Armenians from the Holly Sea of Saint Ecmiadzin visited Ethiopia upon the invitation of His Holiness Abune Paulos the Patriarch of the Ethiopian Orthodox Church. The community arranged receptions at the club in the Addis Ababa Hilton, visits to monasteries and churches and an official meeting with the Holy Synod of the Ethiopian Orthodox Church. It was a very well-organized reception for His Holiness and the three Archbishops, the bishop, and the deacon accompanying him. Everything went smoothly until the Holy Mass, towards the end of mass, the Catholicos became restless, and just when the Bishop turned to give the sermon, Karekin II gathered his entourage to leave the church. I saw that the AGBU clan also followed the move. Abune Paulos called me in despair asking what was happening. Not only could I not explain, but I was speechless. I was not aware of a clandestine meeting between the AGBU and the beneficiary of the AGBU, Karekin II. Abune Paulos told me I was hoping to take the holy communion from him. What happened there was sacrilege for the Ethiopian Orthodox Church.

We stopped the mass, saw the dignitaries off, and Archbishop Zaven Chinchinian and I reentered the church to continue the worship. After the luncheon reception, a group was in the lobby of the Hilton, when suddenly out of the blue, Karekin II turned to me and in front of the crowd scolded me saying, "it would have been better if you had given away the church, instead of committing blasphemy," referring to church services I officiated. The accusation threw me off my feet – I was furious. For the first time in my life, I referred to clergy in the singular. "Unlike you, I do not give away this church, and I serve this church not for a benefit but as a believer. You took the cloak for convenience; I do it for my faith. Overall this makes me a better Christian than you will ever be. I added in anger if you are so concerned, cancel your flight tonight and re-bury over a hundred individuals for whom I have performed funeral services. He didn't expect this outburst from me, surprised by it, he tried to change the subject. It was dead silence, Archbishop Zaven Chinchinian, who ordained me twenty or more years back, could not open his mouth, he was in shock too. Only Bedros Aslanian said Your Holiness, while you were giving presents to everyone including the drivers, you did not even give him a small cross made of copper, is this how you give recognition to persons who serve the church? I left the group and went home, remembering the incident that happened in 1965 when His Holiness Vazken I, gave the Nerses Shnorhali medal he brought for my father to someone else who donated US Dollars 5,000 to Echmiadzin. It is a sad reality that the "Krikor Lousavorich" and the "Nerses Shnorhali" honors of Echmiadzin are for sale. Karekin

II holds a grudge against me to this date. With my unparalleled service, at least a consideration honoring me with one would have been appropriate, but at this stage, I will not even accept one if ever offered. I am not after earthly honors.

The accusation of blasphemy by Karekin II is also wrong because as a deacon I am ordained to serve the church: and church means the assembly of people in the name of God. As Reverend Dr Giragos Leylekyan explains.

Quote

"THE TWO BIBLICAL OFFICES: ELDERS AND DEACONS

Comparing the office of deacon to the office of elder will help us answer these questions. The primary spiritual leaders of a congregation are the elders, who are also called overseers or pastors in the New Testament. Elders teach or preach the Word and shepherd the souls of those under their care (Eph. 4:11; 1 Tim. 3:2; 5:17; Titus 1:9; Heb. 13:17). Deacons, too, have a crucial role in the life and the health of the local church, but their role is different from the elders'. The biblical role of deacons is to take care of the physical and logistical needs of the church so that the elders can concentrate on their primary calling.

This distinction is based on the pattern found in Acts 6:1–6. The apostles were devoted "to prayer and the ministry of the word" (v. 4). Since this was their primary calling, seven men were chosen to handle more practical matters to allow the apostles the freedom to continue with their work.

This division of labor is similar to what we see with the offices of elder and deacon. Like the apostles, the elders' primary role is one of preaching the Word of God. Like the seven, deacons serve the congregation in whatever practical needs may arise."

Unquote

The 24th of April 2015 was the Centenary of the Armenian Genocide. We as an Armenian Community of survivors decided to mark the occasion. We invited the Khachadourian string quartet,

His Excellency Dr. Armen Melkonian the Ambassador of the Republic of Armenia to Ethiopia and His Grace Bishop Ashot Mnatsakanian the primate of the Armenians of Africa. It was a very well-organized event with the main highlight being the concert followed by the reception.

After my opening speech and the national anthems of both nations, and a toast to Ethiopia and Armenia, the Ambassador made a statement about the Genocide and the implications of its denial.

The following is from my opening speech:

> *"This day we have marked it as a Remembrance Day. And with the remembrance, we, we want to take the opportunity to express our gratitude to the nations who made our survival possible.*
>
> *The remembrance is for all those who perished because of their ethnicity or religion, and all those driven away from their ancestral land and homes, and those who fled the atrocities towards the unknown.*
>
> *And our heartfelt gratitude goes to all those nations and leaders of the countries who had the wisdom and the humanity to give refuge to the Armenian survivors.*
>
> *As Ethiopian Armenians we want to take this opportunity to thank the rulers of Ethiopia who gave a homeland to our ancestors at a time where there was no concept of refugee the way we understand today, no agencies dealing with refugee issues. And yet some humane leaders, without the suggestion of an agency, gave refuge to the Armenians, like Emperor Menelik II, Empress Taytu, Lidj Eyassu, Empress Zewditu, and Emperor Haile Selassie I.*
>
> *On behalf of the Republic of Armenia, the Armenian Orthodox Church and the Armenian Community of Ethiopia I dedicate this concert to the government and the entire Ethiopian Nation.*
>
> *Let us raise our glasses to toast for the prosperity, peace, and stability of The Federal Democratic Republic of Ethiopia and the Republic of Armenia."*

An Ethiopian scholar approached me during the reception, and he said – it is Ethiopia that must thank the Armenians for their contribution.

This sentence was the culmination for the years I dedicated to the community.

I was hesitant to write this chapter because it strongly reflects the central role my family and I had in directing the Ethiopian Armenians through the dark periods of Ethiopia. There are those who will be appreciative of what we have done and those who would criticize it, but there will be no one who would be able to deny the truth. I can write about the joys and heartaches we experienced during this selfless sacrifice for the community, but in this book, I will refrain from going into more detail. The only sentence I want to write is to my family.

I thank all of you, Mary, Salpi, Garen, Elise, Raffi, Arakel and Hermine for your unconditional trust and support to fulfill my dreams for the revival and survival of the community.

CHAPTER FOURTEEN

In 1974, Marxist dictator Mengistu overthrew Haile Selassie, Ethiopia's last emperor.

In the end, it was a combination of things that led to the weakening of of Emperor Haile Selassie's rule in the early 1970s and his eventual downfall in 1974. As calls for change by students, the military and some members of the ruling family came, Emperor Haile Selassie's efforts to modernize the country's education system combined with his decreasing mental awareness led to his fall in 1974. Mengistu Haile Mariam ousted him from power keeping him in a dungeon until he died in 1975. The official announcement was that he died of natural causes, but later evidence shows that he was strangled to death on Mengistu's orders.

Emperor Haile Selassie was a strong leader who, over four decades instituted a new constitution, centralized his power and brought reforms that would modernize Ethiopia by strengthening schools and the police.

As he grew less mentally alert, the Emperor started to make errors in judgment and misplaced his trust in an ambitious and manipulative nobleman with his eye on the throne. According to rumors, this nobleman had a generations-old family feud with Emperor Haile Selassie. So while Mengistu ordered the assassination of all high ranking officials and nobleman, the Dejazmaxh was not among them. And when he died of natural causes, his funeral was of royal standard. There were many rumors about the relationship with Mengistu, which go beyond my scope.

Immediately following Haile Selassie's downfall, the Derg, the military junta, took over the streets and started enforcing new laws. The Derg was established from several Ethiopian armed forces, and they implemented policies for the country such as land distribution, nationalizing industries, and services under public ownership, and leading the country into Socialism.

For forty years blame for the failure of the revolution in Ethiopia was placed on the policies of Emperor Menelik II and Emperor Haile Selassie I, but the downfall started on the November 23, 1974 two months after the fall of Emperor Haile Selassie. The Massacre of the Sixty that took place on the morning of 23 November 1974 when the Derg executed 60 imprisoned former government officials at Kerchele prison was the sudden death of the hope that Ethiopia's revolution could be bloodless. The Derg lost the people at this juncture.

There were some Ethiopians who wanted the change and others who did not like the Haile Selassie regime, but they revered it. Only the Derg wanted their blood.

The Derg ruled seventeen years, and it was seventeen years of perpetual decline for this country and the regime. The planned assassination of the sixty officials was the first of a series of many mistakes that followed, proving that Mengistu and his advisors did not know Ethiopia and they did not understand the Ethiopian mentality. The Ethiopian patience and indifference wore on the regime until the end. In interviews, Mengistu blames this shameful act on the 600 participants of infamous forced meeting of all the Derg members, who voted for the death of the 60 high ranking officials and to date denies his involvement in the decision contrary to his colleague's memoirs.

Another crucial mistake was all the attention the Derg put on the internal power struggle and the period of terror and political assassinations. The vacuum created by the conflict in Arat Kilo made Ethiopia vulnerable to external forces who infiltrated Ethiopia. The clear objective of these forces was to divide Ethiopia by helping the secession of Eritrea and fulfilling the centuries-old dream of turning the Red Sea into an Arab lake and to destabilize the Horn of Africa for a hidden agenda. Libya, Algeria, Syria, Iraq, and others behind these forces gave their wholehearted support to the Eritrean Liberation Front which was predominantly an Islamic group, which got financing and and weapons. At that critical moment, Mengistu upon the instigation of the Arab group in the OAU, severed relations with Israel. The United States of America was also leaving Ethiopia on its own.

In his speech on one of his last days, Mengistu claimed sarcastically, "I spread gold under your feet, and you thought it was manure." What he didn't realize or care about is that, unlike manure that fertilizes the land for growth and better crop, his reign, had no positive qualities whatsoever. His rule brought famine, forced displacement, persecution, terror and paying for the bullet that killed your loved one. Inhumane acts that have no absolution for the public.

Many scholars argue that the ruling class owned all the land, but this argument is disputable for me as on many occasions we negotiated with the peasants who owned it. The nobles were indisputably the landlords of vast areas. It was not unique to Ethiopia. It is a stark reality that occurred in the development of many countries during times of strife and political unrest, even in very modern exemplary countries. "Land to the tiller" the infamous, ideology spread in the University, was only a propaganda tool and subject of provocation. It appeals to the idealistic students and the masses. In reality though, "land to the tiller" by itself is not and cannot be a solution. It is, in fact, the reason for impoverishment. The only agriculture that can raise the faith of Ethiopia is one that appropriates capital for full mechanization and commercial farming. The peasant lost everything when the government took over as a landlord and placed them under cooperatives with nothing in the end. And with EPRDF the land and vast areas are leased to foreign companies, which will not benefit Ethiopia at all. The remaining small piece of land divided between children was insignificant and insufficient to crop even for their use. The approach to the rural policy of villagization of the Derg also failed, as it did not take into account the mentality and the culture and tradition. Of course, the farmworker resisted, and the forceful dislocation increased discontent amongst the people. Mengistu didn't care. In one of his speeches, Mengistu criticized the committee that did not implement the policies correctly. Admittedly, the idea behind the program in itself had some potential even though the method used for the implementation was brutal.

Driving through rural Ethiopia what I always observe and comment on is the distance from one end to the other of the villages, mostly developed alongside the highway with a few household widths on both sides of the road, creating communities that stretch for ten to twenty, and even more kilometers. The development and control of such places is a tough task for any government, with regards to providing healthcare, education, utilities, municipal services and social and cultural events for the population in this type of township. Towns need a center. The difficulty to get from one place to another and the waste of time and resources for movement within the towns hinders development and delays progress.

My belief is, and common sense shows, that communities with a town center thrive. With access to a school, church, and mosque, hospital, an organized marketplace, and a town-hall with a multi-purpose auditorium on one side of the road about a kilometer from the highway and a roadside for providing service to people passing through it, there is a possibility for growth. Undoubtedly that simplifies the connection of the area to the power grid, water supply and telecommunications. Villages emerge that will grow into cities, and the pressure on the capital will ease up, and development will disperse over the entire country. And I also believe that responsibility to put these structures in place belongs to the government.

The agricultural policy of the Derg also alienated the population of the country. The staple food of Ethiopia is "injera." I remember lengthy debates about the disadvantages of tef and the propaganda about maize; the culture for eating corn is more or less an amusement rather than nutrition in Ethiopia. The growth of tef gave way to maize resulting in the price hike on the main staple food of the country, and the scarcity of it forced the people to shift to wheat bread. A country self-sufficient with its staple food became dependent on imported wheat, and this created an unnecessary burden on the government, creating dependence on foreign aid. Bakeries producing bread that mostly catered to the external community could no longer meet the demand, causing bread queues. Maize in no way turned into a staple food for Ethiopia. Due to various factors, the production of oilseeds also decreased, creating a shortage thus making Ethiopia dependent on imported oil. I remember that in our house we used only imported olive oil for salad dressing. All the rest of the cooking was with locally produced oil, and there were many small presses all over the town from where you could buy any quantity worth twenty-five cents up to a full barrel. The policy of the Derg was hemmed on mega projects that all failed; I always told my customers who sought advice from me, "a child is born small and grows big if you give birth to a massive child the mother suffers or even dies." The small entrepreneur will become a manufacturer and eventually an industrialist, following the pattern of natural growth. The centralized policy made all these small initiatives disappear, and in the end, there was no oil. Oil was therefore rationed, adding again another stress for the population.

Up to now the majority of edible oil is imported or is donated by foreign governments surely with strings attached. In the old days, a household bought injera at 25 cents apiece, paid a similar amount for oil which would last for two days and some "shiro" and was able to prepare a meal for the family. The Derg policies squashed these possibilities. I recall explanations about the production of oranges. The existing farms and orchards produced excellent quality local oranges and grapefruit enough for the country and enough for export. The government decided to add value by cultivating Jaffa oranges for which purposes they cut all the existing fruit-bearing trees and created an orange shortage for a few years until it was reversed. I remember that to buy oranges you were forced to buy bananas too during this time. The sad part is that the orange trees introduced by the Derg to this day still produce small, dry and substandard oranges. We had the local fruit, but the Derg, in its infinite wisdom wanted to recreate it, which is a typical socialistic revolutionary attitude.

The military, especially those deployed in the North were tired and dissatisfied. One evening sitting in the restaurant of the Hotel Ambasoira in Asmara a few generals next to my table, unaware of my knowledge of Amharic, were discussing their difficulties and the impossible commands from Addis Ababa. I saw the despair in their eyes and fatigue on the faces. At one point I called the waiter over and in a loud, clear voice using Amharic, I asked for bread. This was my way of alerting them that I know the language. They continued to complain undeterred.

A few months after the incident in the restaurant, Mengistu said about his commanders in the North: "I poked their buttocks with the bayonet." Mengistu thoroughly enjoyed publicly humiliating and demeaning his generals. He used his authority to demoralize an already unmotivated army whose salaries were chronically delayed. The soldiers stopped fighting; some defected towards the rebel forces if accepted or otherwise fled the country. The dissatisfaction of the soldiers was another reason for the revolution, and now within a few years, the soldier was not only hungry and without proper uniform but was also at the mercy of the almighty for his life in danger.

I had to visit Asmara Brewery for a sales call together with the salesman from Henkel in charge of Ethiopia. There was no restriction to fly to Asmara, but to take the flight back to Addis Ababa required permission. We could only stay one day in Asmara, so I left my guest with the German brew master of Melotti, taking his passport, and my ID card and went to get our permit to return to Addis Ababa the next morning. Near the municipality building in a room adjacent to the road was the permit granting office. I queued up with about forty persons ahead of me when suddenly heavy shooting started. Near a jewelry shop just opposite the municipality, I saw someone drop. The person in front of me pulled me towards the main entrance of city hall. I followed him, the guards were closing the doors, but they opened it for me, taking me for a foreigner, we entered thus returning the favor to my savior. We hid for over an

"I Want to Die with a Flag"

hour in the building until the battle subsided. After all that, I got the permits we needed.

My next destination was to the airline office to reconfirm the tickets. After an hour's wait, I approached the counter only to hear that dignitaries would be traveling on our flight, so we were being pushed to the next day's flight out. After a lengthy argument, I managed to get seats for my German colleague and me on the small plane that flew the historical route – Asmara, Axum, Mekele, Lalibela, Gonder, Bahar Dar, Debre Markos and with an extra stop at Motta. I arrived at in Addis Ababa eight hours later. Going to Asmara airport while waiting for our taxi to arrive, U.S. Embassy cars came to pick up few Americans whom I met in Asmara quite often, I knew who they were, but they did not know me, and I am sure I was bumped off because of them. Except for Mekele, Bahar Dar and Gonder, it was an experience watching the donkeys and the cattle driven away from the grass for our landing with the Douglass DC3.

When I contemplated how I would write this book, I had considered writing a historical account of the Armenians in Ethiopia. After long deliberation, I realized such a task would put me in the category of the lot producing yet another myth and adding one more to those that already exist. This prospect was not attractive to me. Many scholars follow a specific agenda, and they tell the story pursuing it, missing the essence which is to impart the experience of a specified period for the benefit of future generations. Finally, I decided to write about my personal experiences, through which I hope to shed some insight into those periods without any hidden objective, based entirely on personal understanding and beliefs.

The Derg lacked political maturity, and they vastly underestimated the enemy throughout their reign. Contrary to the Ethiopian character of suspicion around the simplest greeting of an oncoming person, the Derg took action based on hasty emotions and without analyzing the consequences. During the last few years of the Derg, I followed the TPLF radio and other rebel news with great attention, the confirmation of which would come from the Ethiopian

Television news while negating the information. When the rebel radios said they took over a village, the Ethiopian Television said the government inaugurated a school in that same village. It was up to the listener to decipher the truth from a lie. On many occasions, while following the broadcasts, I realized that there was a message or a provocation directed towards the government, and the rebels wanted the government to react so that they achieved a military strategy. When rumors fed to Legesse Asfaw, presenting Hawsen as bait, without any counterintelligence clarification, the government bombed the market, where a professional camera crew filmed it and gave it to the western media, showing the atrocities of a government against an unsuspecting civilian population. The thousands of innocent victims were caught up between two unconscientious parties. The footage shifted all foreign aid to the rebels. Don't believe everything you hear on "the news." Much of it is altered, biased, and marketed to tell a different story from what is true.

In 1989 the Derg realized that their path of socialism was a complete failure, so they started to loosen the tight grip they had on the economy, encouraging private parallel investment. During that period, many industries; shoewear production, printing, plastic, and soap were developed. Many investors, specially the ones with insider information, did very well during this period, taking advantage of the foreign currency allocations for the import of machinery and raw materials by the European Union, and the Italian Co-operation Agency. Otherwise, the government was bankrupt, and my business was affected tremendously. I spent most of 1988 in London helping the head-office on other markets and training personnel. When Mary faced complications in the later months of pregnancy to our third child Raffi, she had to remain under observation, so we flew to Canada and stayed with my mother for about three months. After Raffi's birth in Canada on the 10th of October 1988, when the snow started falling the beginning of November, we flew back to Addis Ababa via London.

Another mistake of the Derg was changing the historically divided administrative borders within Ethiopia. Based on a century-old experience of monarchs, the divisions of administrative boundaries were strategically divided and not purely ethnically or linguistically. The Derg eliminated Begiemder and Semaine and brought it under a loose Gonder administration creating a vacuum zone in the North of Ethiopia. Other voids emerged in the west with Illubabor and Kaffa, and east in the Afar region, and the south-east of the country with Harerge and Ogaden. Consulting history for reasons of dividing zones and administrative areas, whether for geographic, ethnic, linguistic or strategic is an absolute necessity. There was a strategic reason that Addis Ababa was in Shewa which became apparent for the EPRDF once it wanted to expand the capital to cover a territory with a radius of 120 kilometers around it. If they had any respect for history, Shewa would be on the map, and they could realize the desired expansion of Addis Ababa, within Shewa.

Fortified by the imminent fall of the Derg and following the concept "strike when the iron is hot," we took advantage of the relaxed process for investment and invested in two new projects. The approval for a shoe component production and that of a leather tannery came very fast. Following the advice of elders, we chose the nationalized land in Bishoftu that belonged to our father previously, within few days we got the factory area, with an apology from the administrator of Adaa region about the destruction of the once manicured gardens. The remnants of our old house and some water towers showed that a government should concentrate on an army, look after the security of the country, engage in diplomacy, regulate the laws and collect taxes. Anything else is the job of the private sector.

The only commendable points of the Derg were the transparency and the partial independence of the legal system and the opportunity created for many to become homeowners. The beginnings of the massification of education were also laudable even though the quality of education suffered for this decision. Once Mengistu realized the unknown ideology that they followed failed, he tried to improve some laws, but it was much too little and much too late.

Mengistu brought in an American Company, Hunt Oil, and rumors had it that they rediscovered the oil in Ethiopia. Was history repeating itself for the third time?

The Derg hijacked the popular revolution which was instigated by a few radical students and professors with no real agenda and as a result sailed the country through a misguided, destructive, bloody era. The 120 members of the Derg and its 600 person secondary junta, raised their hands for the blood of people like Iskender Desta who was not even in Ethiopia, some raised it from the thirst of blood, others because of fear and some to appease Mengistu.

All in all, the Derg's reign of terror caused unnecessary conflict and war. They imprisoned, then executed 60 former government officials, crushing any hope that this regime would be bloodless. The Derg that claimed to be in control of the country and mother nature, as displayed on a banner which remained on the gate of the palace for many years to come but failure after failure resulted in their feared leader being the first to jump ship. The Derg could not even represent Ethiopia in the meeting that decided Ethiopia's future in London.

On the last days of the Derg, the atmosphere in Addis Ababa was tense despite the peaceful retreat of the soldiers. The palace strengthened its defenses and even placed tanks on the small roads that led to the residence and offices of Mengistu. As Mengistu boasted he was going to defend the capital to the last drop of his blood, we expected fierce fighting. We saw a tank and armored vehicle approach our house and park strategically. A battle in front of our house seemed imminent. The schools closed, the shops opened shorter hours, and the empty shelved groceries sold their remaining stocks. We stocked up on water, flour, yeast, and as it is a tradition for our family, we had a substantial quantity of bulgur wheat that could carry us for some time in case we were trapped at home. Besides doing the inventory of the food supply, we made preparations for reinforcing the windows, the front doors and the gate of the compound. The tension and anticipation of something of great danger affected both Garen and Elise, who asked many questions and we tried to keep them calm. Raffi was a baby and his milk supply was secure thanks to my office in London, our diplomatic friends and the elderly members of our community, who queued up to take their ration of powdered milk to give to us.

Half a million-armed soldiers passed through Addis Ababa and yet no one was hurt. While they could have taken anything by force, they asked only for food, water, and direction. I transported a few of them to the train station when I found them in front of my office asking for directions. I admired their discipline and politeness. On this same day, half of Los Angeles burnt because of police brutality. A relative calling from Los Angeles to ask if we were safe, my reply was, you have to worry about your safety, Ethiopians are peaceful people by nature. Los Angeles police brutality and "Operation Solomon" overshadowed the historical events unraveling in Ethiopia. Thirty-five Israeli Hercules planes transported the Ethiopian Jews of Bete Israel, including the name of a trusted advisor to Mengistu, who boarded the last flight.

Mengistu traded with the powers-that-be for his escape by allowing for the expatriation of the Ethiopian Jews of Bete Israel.

CHAPTER FIFTEEN

In his last televised parliament meeting, President Mengistu tried appeasing the people and the country watched on as the Derg, including civilians, scholars and even clergy rose in the endless assembly. I was not there but what we saw televised and heard were the famous stories from that time was the incident where a priest addressed Mengistu telling him:

"I hope that like Emperor Theodoros, you will remain on that chair until you are "qwanta" (a cured piece of meat (jerky)."

To which Mengistu replied,

"I assure you I will be here up to the moment a bullet cracks open my forehead."

As history attests these words proved to be cowardly rhetoric. After all, Mengistu now lives in Zimbabwe; he is hardly in Ethiopia, but I digress. So as the Derg fell, Mengistu had an Imperial Rolls Royce driven onto a plane, and he fled to Harare where the ambassador was a close relative of his, and the country remained without a leader for over fifteen days from the time of Mengistu's escape. The discipline of the Addis Ababa population was exemplary, showing how capable people are of handling themselves responsibly making you wonder about the extreme: do people need governments, if they can behave themselves without its presence?

Then the EPRDF came in, and a new chapter in Ethiopia's history started. The new beginning had snags connected with the replacement of the century-old symbol of Ethiopia with a communist-inspired red and yellow flag, a clear demonstration of an occupying force conquering enemy territory. The flag replacement at Menelik II square was what angered Ethiopians most. The first action of our new leader, before he addressed the country was to talk to the ones who helped him get that position, confirming his priorities. Ethiopians who were secondary listened to the repetitive phrase that a "flag is a piece of cloth." This alienated him from Ethiopians. Patience, indifference and the deep belief that God protects Ethiopia went into action. The support of the Western Countries kept the TPLF in power until the internal coup of the parliament in 2018, which luckily preceded a potential genocide. It is interesting though for me as both an Ethiopian and an Armenian. A revolution in Armenia in 2018 toppled the ruling party, and they called it "The velvet revolution," inspiring me to view the one in Ethiopia in much the same way and call it "The silky coup."

Salpi panicked though after listening to the first speech of Meles Zenawi. She had a premonition remembering some of her cellmates in the "mahakelawi," and she lost her calm. She predicted chaos and division. And just as she predicted committees started forming, and others were created to control that committee and bureaucracy grew without limitations. She wasn't wrong; chaos was about to come.

Back in 1975 the literacy campaign successfully dispersed the students all over the country, using their idealism to serve the country. The aim of the Derg was not purely to teach the population how to read and write, but it was to disperse the revolutionary students away from the comfort of the University base. Once Mengistu approved of the assassination of the sixty, many of the dispersed revolutionaries realized the hijacking of their revolution by the military. This time their task was to topple a military regime, so they did not return and instead, found fertile ground to grow into a front in the bosom of the strongly supported Islamic Eritrean Liberation Front. The ELF needed distractions for the Ethiopian Army. The TPLF was one and EPLF the Christian faction of the ELF was the second. The TPLF comprised of three camps, the Marxist, the Idealists, and the Ethnic Nationalists. The integration and the elimination of the Marxist wing, left idealists expanding and organizing the front, while the opportunistic Ethnic Nationalists gradually infiltrated into the higher ranks and took over the front. The remnants of EPRP also joined them, and after some training, they opened yet another front against the Ethiopian army.

The first few years of struggle for the TPLF was a difficult period of just barely trying to survive, relying mostly on handouts from the ELF and plundering the few animals and food from the relatively better off farmers in the region. The looting of the Commercial Bank Branches initially was unsuccessful, and the one attempt in Adua does not render any complimentary words about the revered visionary leader. In 1983, Derg imprisoned some Tigreans in the government offices under the suspicion of espionage and supporting the rebel groups. Among the confined, there were a few from wealthy families, who despised the rebels more than the government because of atrocities done by the rebels to their families, and in Addis Ababa. Because of their ethnicity, they had to endure torture and unknown periods in jail without due process of law, caught between two evils. There were also active agents of the rebels in town who collected money to send to the TPLF, and the government was determined to crack down the chain.

In March 1984 the Ethiopian government was preparing for an elaborate celebration for its tenth-anniversary, It spent money on arches, a concert hall, an office building for the president, a new house for Mengistu with a swimming pool, a military parade venue, a martyrs monument and many more. All this lavish wasteful use of money while millions of Ethiopians were on the verge of starvation. In his book and in interviews when asked, Mengistu downplays it to a single memorial built by North Korea, which features his profile. Did he consider the population as deaf, dumb and blind idiots who understand nothing? The lack of rain and predictions of continuing dryness caused aid organizations to appeal to governments, who showed reluctance in supporting a brutal regime.

Nevertheless, they put more pressure and called on the public and collected millions of dollars; Band-Aid released an album

"Do They Know It's Christmas" and the profits were directed to Ethiopia. "Live Aid." Other organized concerts raised millions for Ethiopia. I always wondered what the author of the award-winning documentary film "The Unknown Famine" thought when he witnessed the outcome of his award-winning achievement; instead of a hundred thousand victims which he portrayed in the film, there were a million and more victims. That fame cost and is still costing millions of lives in Ethiopia – after all how many more unknown humanitarian emergencies has Ethiopia seen since then? Unknown to the world but hardly unknown to the now millions of displaced, hungry and vulnerable people.

In 1985 the aid organizations infiltrated the rebel-held areas and negotiated directly with the rebels. The TPLF used most of the money received directly from them and even sold the grain received from the aid organizations to aid organizations and neighboring countries and used all the income on armaments, ammunition, professional cameras, communication equipment, and wireless telephones. Famine was on sale. Foreign diplomats talked with admiration about the communication and discipline of the rebels in those days. In the end, the foreigners diverted the majority of the aid to the rebels, or so I was told by some of these foreigners. Addis suffered from food scarcity and depended on the foreign handouts. We received baby formula from friends and relatives abroad through our contacts. The shortages for petrol, bread, meat, rice, sugar, milk, fruits, baby formula, and toilet papers needed an extra employee to just queue-up.

On the 11th of May 1991, a diplomat friend of mine came to Bishoftu, where every Saturday we, together with the family, followed the progress of the construction work of our projects. We lunched together, and for the first time, he started asking the names of the mountains around. Was there a hidden message? I jokingly told him – have the rebels conquered the hills? There was no reply.

We received our machinery in Djibouti a few days earlier. Bringing it to the compound was an experience of epic proportions. The chronic shortage of trucks, all directed towards the famine and the

"I Want to Die with a Flag"

war effort, forced us to ship the machinery from Europe to Djibouti, instead of Assab. We were in a hurry to get it on the site before the anticipated change of government. Using all our contacts we had the cargo loaded on a train from Djibouti to Addis Ababa. These arrived at the railway customs, but the clearance was in Adama, 100 kilometers away. Instead of doing the tours of the offices in Addis Ababa we drove three times to Adama in one day. Finally, we managed to complete the clearance and started looking for a truck. The announcement of the government obliging all truck owners to standby for deployment to wherever the government assigned them, made it impossible for us to find even dump trucks to transport our stuff. Finally, we contacted the governor of the Adaa district, who gave us a name and a number in the Air Force Base headquarters in Bishoftu, telling us the officer might be able to help us. And in fact, he did.

The Air Force provided us with an old Soviet truck and promised to unload it in the factory with their crane as well. As arranged, the car arrived early morning in Addis Ababa and loaded the equipment from the Addis Ababa customs and left for Bishoftu. We followed him to Bishoftu after we made sure that it was in the factory. We went to the gate of the Air Force to direct the crane to our compound. But by lunchtime, the government announced the closing of all businesses, shops and government offices for the televised speech of President Mengistu. That was the famous speech in which he said his famous sentence, "I presented gold to the people of Ethiopia, but they saw it as dung," his farewell to Ethiopia. Anyway, we waited for the crane with little hope, but there was no movement at the Air Force, the truck was stuck in our compound. Late in the afternoon we went to the factory and observed the driver moving out of the factory. We stopped him; he explained that he could not leave the truck out of the Air Force compound, as it was out only for the day. We understood his problem, he went. Salpi and I returned to Addis Ababa, without talking, afraid of unleashing the "what if" questions. With no prior discussion we set in the car at 6:30 in the morning, and by 7:15 we were at the gate of the Air Force base with fear and anticipation, to follow the truck and the crane. The Soviet-made crane showed up at about 9:00 am, but there was no sign of the lorry with our goods on it. We tried asking, but no one was aware of the described vehicle coming in the previous evening. After an hour of inquiries, we decided to go to the factory, to our surprise and delight, we saw the truck and the crane trying to coordinate the unloading. The driver understood our apprehension, and so on the previous evening, he parked the car at the second gate of the Air Force base to leave the compound without having to go through the usual red-tape. The one "fleshing machine" weighed 7,000 kilograms. It took a while to unload it, and Mary was not happy at how late we got back to Addis Ababa.

On 24th of May 1991, Israel started the evacuation of the Ethiopian Jews, and most embassies remained with skeleton personnel. We needed to pay the employees in Bishoftu, and when we phoned the district administrator, his response was – come early, do what you have to do, and leave immediately. The route was spooky silent as there was not a soul moving; even the animals grazing did not cross the roads. Within half an hour we were in the compound, and after twenty minutes, we left for Addis Ababa. Our neighbor, a retired air force colonel, told us – you go now! I will help your foreman. All the guards abandoned the factory beforehand to be with their families, leaving the foreman alone in the large compound.

There was a wedding the next day and reception in Bishoftu on Sunday, the father of the bride asked Salpi to sing the Ave Maria at the Church. She agreed. Life goes on. A friend came by as we were practicing Salpi's singing, and he laughed at the absurdity of the situation; everyone in Addis was bracing for the descent into madness, and there we were practicing the Ave Maria.

While life continued even in the midst of instability and even though we remained calm, I did advise the father of the bride to cancel the reception as Bishoftu was already under rebel control. Uncertainty took over his expression; probably he thought – "why this weekend?" In the beginning, he was not keen on the idea of the cancelation, but the next day he did cancel it. A German television crew crashed the wedding reception in the Hilton, with their cam-

"I Want to Die with a Flag"

eras, in search of a controversy, to show their audience that people unaware or careless of the events in the country are in celebration. Organizing weddings takes more than one day or a week. I avoided the cameras and cautioned the father of the bride to ask them to put down the cameras. He did, but the next day friends from Germany seeing many acquaintances, phoned us giving the details of the broadcast. Just as I expected, this revealed that diplomats and foreign communities are unaware and indifferent to the changes happening. I was not, the diplomats were not, and indeed, none of the international communities were unresponsive to the changes but what to do.

Our factory neighbor called on Sunday assuring us that everything was starting to settle down. Soldiers visiting the area cautioned our foreman not to open the gate for any unauthorized person. The rebel coalition forces entered Addis Ababa on the 28th of May 1991 under the name of Ethiopian People's Revolutionary Democratic Front. The name is still used up to now, despite a few of the words being obsolete for over twenty years, and I believe that renaming the party is timely now. Their entry on that day interested me a lot when I saw the Israeli trained special forces of Mengistu jump over the fence of the palace in their pajamas and pretend to be passersby to escape arrest. These were ruthless soldiers, who abused the Arat Kilo neighborhood, especially the girls of the "seven doors," seven small night joints between our house and the palace. I was witnessing yet another regime change.

Following the advice of ill-informed and biased intelligence operatives in Ethiopia, Mr. Herman Cohen of the State Department delivered Ethiopia to the ethnic nationalists, camouflaged under the banner of EPRDF. It was undeniable that at that moment the rebel coalition was a well-organized minority group, but what the "London Meeting" completely ignored was that they could not represent the Ethiopian people. Did Mr. Cohen have a mandate from the people of Ethiopia to give "state responsibility"? Ethiopia and its people remain thankful to all who intervened and circumvented a bloody war to the end. We should not also forget that the army stopped fighting long before the occupation of Addis Ababa and the transfer of power to a minority in London. The method was not at all democratic; it was an imposition on the people of Ethiopia, equivalent to a colonial appointment in the 19th century.

When I hear the word democracy, it confuses me. Democracy is the most overused, abused, and confusing word, that has lost its meaning in reality. Dictators use it; despots use it, all parties opposing and insulting each other use it, making the word meaningless. It no longer reflects the people's wishes if it ever has. Does it ever become the rule of the people? Even with the champions of democracy, this word loses its meaning when a popular vote is just a statistical number.

Mr. Cohen announced in London "No democracy, no cooperation." Did the west witness any democracy to continue the cooperation for so many years? I doubt if they even looked for the rule of the people when flooding aid to Ethiopia. Again, I included, the people of Ethiopia are thankful for all the support, but the "No democracy, no cooperation" principal was a farce looking at the results of the elections which were as democratic as the ones during the Derg.

In the London meeting, Ato Meles Zenawi promised to transfer Ethiopia into a "no democracy country," what did Mrs. Ana Gomes have to say about this? I wonder after her leadership over the 2005 European Union Electoral Observation mission with top-level government officials personally maligned for. In that same speech, Ato Meles Zenawi announced "an end to starvation, an end to conflicts within the country." Promises to this date remain unfulfilled.

There was no resistance in Addis Ababa, but the EPRDF forces once more demonstrated that they conquered enemy territory and, to deprive the enemy with firepower, managed to blow-up ammunition depots causing damage to a vast area, in Addis Ababa and Dukem, a village 35 kilometers from Addis Ababa. This act reminded me of an Armenian author Yervant Odian, who describing communist revolutionaries, wrote – "even though the door was open, we broke the window to enter." A curfew was reintroduced, and for over two months we heard gunshots every night to confirm their presence, with flares in the air every hour. The fully armed patrols of the EPRDF soldiers was another phenomenon that was odd to everyone. To me it looked like, they regarded Addis Ababa an enemy territory, and for over ten years roamed around in Addis Ababa and elsewhere, fully armed, with grenades hanging from their belts. Improvised barricades appeared and still exist after twenty-seven years on the pavements near government offices, reminding me of the streets of Asmara during the last years of the Derg. So, while Addis Ababa was their capital – to a certain extent, it also seemed to be the enemy territory. In one speech from the EPRDF leadership, there was an accusation towards the population of Addis Ababa for supporting the old regime, which was not true. The Addis Ababans suffered - not in the same way but life was not easy for anyone in Addis Ababa. And the Addis Ababans weakened the Mengistu regime from within.

After the London appointment, the staged democratic drama, which supposedly represented the whole country, they formed the provisional government, agreeing on the disunion of Eritrea within three years following a referendum. At the time it seemed the entire objective of the meeting was the separation of Eritrea. Some opportunistic groups who joined the coalition and supported in the beginning understood that they had no place in the system deployed. The multiparty umbrella was a fake. It was a single party with multiethnic subdivisions. Even the multiethnicity being doubtful and questioned by Ethiopians, because of the pseudonyms of the party leaders used during the time of struggle. The meeting also revealed that the country would adopt "Ethnic Federalism" as a system to put an end to the conflicts within Ethiopia; The "Ethnic Nationalists," were to exercise "Ethnic Federalism." Ethiopia was the guinea pig for this type of governance. The meeting confirmed the appointment of Ato Meles Zenawi as the president of the Provisional Government.

The first trip the new president took was to Egypt, to which he gave patrolling rights over the Nile river. At the time I thought it was a premature act, but now I think he had the mandate to do so from those who put him in power. Ato Meles was clearing his future path, building their confidence. He also was an expert in handling the Western politicians using words that sounded like a lullaby to them. He was like a chameleon changing his colors to the mood of the environment, a brilliant strategist. He talked to all the world leaders with confidence and conviction but stammered and kept his gaze away from a simple Ethiopian interviewing him in Amharic. In the parliament with the absolute majority, he did not stutter while addressing the assembly in Amharic. The OLF (Oromo Liberation Front) jumped on the London wagon, but when the coalition formed the EPRDF, the OLF realized that OPDO with their butterfly leader, whose ethnicity was a subject of contemplation for the grapevine, sidetracked them. There were also other extremist opportunists who made themselves available to the first meeting, securing some crucial positions for a while.

To eliminate the influence of the majorities represented by the Oromiffa and Amarhic speaking population of the country, the TPLF devised methods of distraction for them. They pushed the Latin alphabet on the Oromos. And imposing the guilty conscience on the Amharas, for having ruled the country and overlooking the fact that the last two monarchs were not pure Amharas and the one preceding was a pure Tigrean. They managed to send the Oromos into a linguistic euphoria to ascertain their identity, but in reality, it created three generations of challenges for educating the Oromo youth, who today are less able to get better-paying jobs outside Oromia competitively. To me, this looked to be the aim of the TPLF. If it indeed was, it backfired on them years later.

As an Armenian, I support the idea of an independent alphabet, if it correctly reflects the sounds of the spoken language. The creation of an alphabet is a complex evolutionary process developed gradually or created scientifically. Unfortunately, the adapted alphabet for Oromifa is neither of the two. It is a feeble creation developed by one with absolutely no idea about linguistics, the esthetics, the sounds required for the language, and the science of alphabets.

In the year 400 AD Catholicos Sahag Bartev of Armenia, gave the task of developing the Armenian alphabet to Messrob Mashdots, who was a visionary and creative individual. Up to then Armenians used the Greek alphabet. In the Armenian language, there are 36 sounds, but the Greek alphabet had only 22 letters initially. Therefore, it was not adequate for the Armenian language. Some of the letters of the Armenian alphabet date back to Kachats Karer (Karahunj), the equivalent of Stonehenge in Armenia. Research done on the source of Armenian letters for centuries was inconclusive and according to Doctor Armenak Yeghiaian, the connection to the Ge'ez alphabet was completely overlooked. His research concludes the possible derivation of at least 17 letters of the Armenian alphabet from figures of the Ge'ez.

Ge'ez	ሀ	ለ	ሎ	ጎ	ቀ	በ	ቡ	ቶ	ኖ	ከ	ደ	ገ	ጠ	ፉ	ፐ	ከ	ቦ
Armenian	Ս	Ղ	Լ	Դ	Փ	Ո	Ռ	Ք	Ն	Ա	Չ	Գ	Ղ	Վ	Մ	Յ	Ր
Equivalent	S	Gh	L	D	P	Vo	RR	K	N	A	Ch	G	B	V	M	J	R

The best source for the interested reader is the published work of Doctor Armenak Yeghiaian in Armenian, in Beirut in 2006 as it is not my intention to research this subject here which is beyond my capability. The reason I diverted from my subject is to debate the issue of how an alphabet is derived. Repetitive figures create confusion and a hindrance to youngsters to read and write other languages which use the Latin alphabet. As additional information to the reader, the Ge'ez alphabet in its final form predates the Armenian alphabet visioned and executed by Messrob Mashdots, at least by fifty years, so questions about Ge'ez using Armenian figures is not probable. There are controversies about the travels of Mesrob Mashdots, whether they include Ethiopia or not, but most sources point it to Ephesus, as the venue where he studied the Ge'ez alphabet. Messrob Mashdots earned sainthood for this invention and for the past sixteen centuries the Armenian people commemorate Saint Messrob day. Therefore, it is not blasphemy to borrow figures, transform them with minimal omissions and additions of lines, rotating to the left or right, or upside down, to achieve perfection, which the Armenian alphabet is. Another note to the reader, Messrob Mashdots preferred straight vertical lines and sculpted the curves on the horizontals.

Beyond the nationalistic explanation given at the time, there was a lame "scientific" reason given for adopting Latin as an alphabet for Oromifa, claiming that thirty-two symbols of the Ge'ez alphabet do not cover all the sounds in Oromifa. There is an anomaly in this argument if thirty-two basic symbols cannot include the sounds of a language how can an alphabet with twenty-six symbols cover all the sounds. Mathematically and logically it is impossible. Therefore, it is normal to conclude that there was an ulterior motive to do so.

The day I heard about the development of an alphabet for Oromifa based on the Latin alphabet I panicked. I visited an influential Oromo friend, to caution him about the linguistic problems that might arise, even jokingly told him to advise the Oromo leaders to consider the Armenian alphabet as an alternative to the Latin as it has thirty-six letters representing the thirty-six sounds in the Armenian language. It seemed the brainwashing also affected his reasoning. To prove the point that it impacts youngsters' ability to learn new languages, I tested many of our employees in Bishoftu and gave them an easy English passage to read. The older generation could recite the words, but the younger generation had difficulty pronouncing English. English is the universal language in the 21st century, depriving generations of that knowledge is a crime.

The worst had yet to come, and that was the creation of the chaos of the educational system. The Ministry of Education divided schooling into four categories, kindergarten, primary, junior secondary and senior secondary and in Oromia, the teaching of English reserved for the top classes. When I was in school, we had Armenian, Amharic, English, and music taught to us from grade one. We did not suffer or feel pressure, to the contrary we actually benefitted by developing the ability to switch between languages with no effort, and that strong base allowed for the learning other subjects and tongues rapidly. The imposition of this system of education is unfair when children of the governing elite attend private international schools who do follow another method of learning.

This double standard proves that the system creators do not believe in their creation. They know that what they devised serves yet another hidden agenda. Journalists challenged Ato Meles Zenawi regarding the capability of officials and his reply was, "even if they are ignorant, as long as they fulfill the party objectives, they are acceptable for me." The party objective and the hidden agenda behind it mattered more than the Ethiopian population, specifically the children who would one day become the youth of today.

After the overthrow of the monarchy, Ethiopia went through difficult times. The reasons for the overthrow continued in the worst manner; freedom of speech and due process of law were denied, human rights were just a fallacy, famine multiplied becoming epidemic. The dream of the transformation of the empire to a republic did not happen. The same division continued between the people and the rulers, but without the savoir-faire of the sovereignty. Mengistu once said, "a lot of people aim for this chair, but only one can sit in it." Unfortunately, Ato Meles once in the "throne," followed many of the paths of his predecessor. He sat on the throne and stepped into the shoes of Mengistu. He perpetuated the same laws, but by using other means and objectives to suppress the population. Neither had the slightest intention of relinquishing that chair. As we say in Armenian "The musicians changed, the same music continued," but this time under self-serving and inexperienced conductors, which the audience grew to despise.

After the Derg, what Ethiopia needed was a transparent government, without any secret aims. Governance and openness was required, not intrigues and hidden agendas and not ethnic divisions. If division is what we are after, then we can find divisibilities, and it is possible to divide even to the single individual, as even identical twins are not the same. The essential factor for the survival of humanity is not division but unity of the people. Integration is strength.

A few months after EPRDF resumed power and felt comfortable, businesses started to move as the foreign aid began to flow in. A customer came to me with a business hunch, there was a shortage of adhesive and asked if we could ship a full container immediately. After agreeing on the price, the goods arrived in Assab. Although all the papers were in order, the clearance became a nightmare. The National Bank of Ethiopia demanded that we include a separate manufacturer's invoice from the one attached to the documents. I contacted them to explain; they turned me down. I saw many experienced suppliers like myself with similar questions. They wanted to build a database for the business-oriented leaders of the country. After six months, companies owned by Ethiopians in Europe started contacting our sources. I sorted out the paperwork, but for "unknown" reasons the problem persisted, and the customer could not bring the item from the port. The goods arrived too late as new importers took control of the market. Alas it was a lost opportunity. Many privates suffered from the preferential treatment of new companies, who gradually controlled most of the the market, belonging to favored cronies and having access to insider information from the National Bank of Ethiopia.

The problems of excessive bureaucracy in Ethiopia started with the Italian occupation, the British completed it, the Haile Selassie régime refined it, the Derg complicated it. The Derg created the dangerous precedence of the directive ruling over the law, the concept of "order from the leadership, and empowerment of the cronies". I traveled to Nairobi every month, so I applied for a border trading license as soon as it opened to the public. I knew I was one of the first to ask for it but I faced a directive, which limited the number of licenses to fifty. The Kiwi producers in Kenya were my clients, and I aimed at importing some shoe polish. After a few days, when I asked for the licenses, they told me that only salt traders have the permission to bring shoe polish. Up to now, I do not see the connection between the two items. The one thing I am sure of is that salt is not an ingredient in the shoe-polish formulation. The cronies of the Derg got all the assigned licenses. These types of limitations marked the beginning of the "insider information" culture that became the dominant business principle for many years to come.

My objective here is to impart my knowledge, understanding, and experience to an interested audience. I will not suppress my opinion regarding the most negative institution in Ethiopia. Usually, central banks are strict and inflexible, but The National Bank of Ethiopia enjoys unlimited power. The National Bank of Ethiopia is the legislator, the judge and jury, the prosecutor and the executor. Such power given to any office opens the gateway to corruption and unhindered control over all the other financial institutions of the country. And because of all these tasks entrusted to them, the accumulation of thousands of conflicting directives and internal guidelines, their duty is obscured. So, any application that goes into that institution is either blocked or neatly filed without a reply. This institution does not function anymore, so much so that they accept painted iron as gold. Or was it the gold of cronies? Either way, I believe in the complete dismantling of the present set-up and re-establishing it from scratch, with an entirely new bloodline A clean start by even renaming it Central Bank of Ethiopia, might stir renewed faith in it and some hope that it stops functioning as the cemetery of Ethiopia's development. During the past forty years, I have not witnessed anything positive issued by them. They issue negative directives, reject all applications indiscriminately, or else it disappears in one of their Bermuda triangles, dead without action or reply. Getting an appointment with the top management is impossible, and in the end, you meet the same familiar faces, who have developed the art of lying to you, that it is a directive, and nothing can change it. "Directives" became the sacred word for the dysfunctional operative to escape responsibility and its status gained a power above the law and even the constitution. Unfortunately, it has created a culture of coverup for the bureaucratic offices.

    I waited a few months after the London conference to go to Asmara for assessing the status of our business. The Ambassoira Hotel, my first choice, turned me down and so did my second choice Nyala Hotel, so finding space in Asmara felt impossible. After a month or so I found a room in a hotel near the industrial area. It was an old Italian colonial villa converted into a hotel; it served my purpose. The minute I arrived there I met a former client, who greeted me in

Italian and offered me a drink, that I regretted to accept. Just as soon as we sat down, he started insulting Ethiopians using derogatory words and this aggravated me. His attack was surprising and his arguments undeserving of an answer. He was on my list of clients that I I had intended to visit but I canceled. I could go back to Addis Ababa the same day as my assessment of future business was evident. Whatever form the business took, Addis Ababa was out of the picture. I changed my plans to seek someone to act as our agent.

Asmara was depleted; the factories were not working everyone had the illusion of dominating business in Ethiopia. When I visited the shops, I saw shoes, shirts and other stuff from Addis Ababa. Their hope to flood the Addis Ababa market with soap, footwear and detergent was an unrealizable dream as the dynamism of business in Addis Ababa was much faster, compared to Asmara. My estimation was that in another six months the euphoria will be over, and markets would move. But I was wrong; until the referendum, it was not over. I appointed an agent to follow our business, trained the office secretaries and the sales personnel and advised the London office to look after the Eritrea business.

Thousands of Eritreans from all over the world flocked into Asmara, and the mood shifted to ecstasy all over the town. The Eritreans were stunned by the idea of freedom which never happened in reality, even after they separated from Ethiopia.

Amharic was taboo, except when alone in an office. I never initiated the Amharic with the thought that I hurt their feelings, but after a minute alone they changed the conversation to Amharic. This was because of the the referendum. The increasing nostalgia of old habits took over the restriction or fear of speaking Amharic. A month before the poll, Asmara was full. The town was in ecstasy, parties everywhere, my thoughts preoccupied trying to imagine the expectation of the people. The main question that occupied my mind was, will these people be ready for the sacrifices a new country will demand from them, after the elimination of the culprit of their misery. Overhearing a conversation, I had a reply; the conviction that because they had, an army, a fleet and the seaports that

"I Want to Die with a Flag"

Ethiopia would depend on them and they would thrive. This did not happen. I liked Asmara and hope that I will have the chance to visit it again one day. My last trip to Asmara made me feel like a teenager whose parents divorced a week ago. That was a disturbing sentiment.

The excitement of the Ethiopian media for the referendum of Eritrea matched and surpassed the jubilation in Asmara; it was the most significant achievement of the government. The coverage dealt as if Ethiopia was casting a vote in the referendum. No predictions or polls were necessary for the outcome, because the question on the ballot was simple, "Freedom" or "Slavery." Whoever devised the ballot paper had a very cynical mentality. Will there be anyone in their right mind choosing slavery over freedom? The answer is a profound NO.

After the referendum, we lost four containers of chemicals imported for our production to the Eritrean government. We never understood what was the reason for this; confiscation or donation? Not only did we lose materials, we also lost the advance payments made for the customs duty and transport expenses. What did EPRDF do? NOTHING. Who was the victim? The Ethiopian taxpayer. The same happened when the war started between the two neighboring countries. This time we lost six containers; it was an enemy property known as "Bene Nemici" in Ethiopia. Did EPRDF take responsibility? No. Who was the victim? The Ethiopian taxpayer.

Belay Negga with whom we became friends while visiting my cousin in prison, had a keen interest in the history of Armenians of Ethiopia. Occasionally upon his request, Mary invited Mr. Avedis Terzian over to dinner, who told him what he knew right down to the minute details of life in the old Harar and Addis Ababa, the development of Addis Ababa, the Italian occupation and other subjects. After Mr. Terzian passed away; Belay Negga occasionally visited us. One day Belay came by unannounced, but it was not a social visit. He asked for a donation for a project in Tigray. My reaction was out of character, and I abruptly said, because you have come, I will give a maximum of Birr 2000 as I do not believe in donations, I prefer creating jobs. He was offended and told me he would not take it and that he was hoping I would give more than my cousin. I also mentioned our confiscated containers in Eritrea for which EPRDF remained indifferent. Discussions on other subjects continued, and unconsciously I offended him again, it was about the Prime Minister. He angrily told me that he shares a grandfather with the PM. A lot of pieces of the jigsaw puzzle found their place in my mind. I still liked Belay, even though he was the one who convicted my uncle to the maximum sentence, he was also the only one to inquire about the court case of my cousin. He knew about my sacrifices during the first case. Our last conversation was on the phone, he asked about the court case, and I gave him a piece of my mind about the legal system. I was sorry to hear about his death a few weeks later.

The first major decision that Eritrea and Ethiopia took, after the separation, was the closure of the petroleum refinery. The reason given was that it was old and economically not feasible. It produced different grades of benzene for vehicles, diesel, kerosene and various classes of tar. The factory was a Soviet refinery built in the early '60s. A British firm a few years earlier concluded a study on renovations of the refinery but, the preference was to close it, add a few hundred more to joblessness, and import the worst quality of fuel into the country. Was that the right decision? No, it was not, and I am sure there are regrets about the decision up to now. The refinery produced two grades of benzene, both of higher octane than the present one imported. Already with the altitude of Addis Ababa, the combustion engines perform below their efficiency, with the added contribution of the very low octane fuel, all cars underperform, contribute to air pollution, reduce the lifespan of the engines, need more maintenance... and I can continue to write a whole separate chapter about it.

There is also another subject worth mentioning. After the Paris conference of Global Warming, Ethiopia announced an unachievable carbon emissions target for the year 2020; Ethiopia imports old cars from Europe, Japan, and the Middle East, that fail the emission criteria in these countries. And yet Ethiopia promised a lower target of carbon emission than these countries. Ethiopia practically became the dump yard of used cars because of a greed-based objective of excessive customs duty imposed by The Inland Revenue and Customs Authority. Import duties that go beyond the price of any duties heard of in the world. In North America, you can buy a brand-new Toyota Camry, with all options, for Birr 600,000. In Ethiopia, you pay the same price for a ten-year-old secondhand Toyota Corolla, with no options, torn tires, a dead battery, rusted exhaust, no catalytic converter and with over 100,000 kilometers on it minimum. It needs renovations the day you buy it. The Toyota model range includes, Corolla, Corona, Carina, and Camry. To buy a new Toyota Corolla in Ethiopia, you'd have to sell your house. The high import duty can translate into human rights violation by the government towards the people. The customs collect a significant sum per car I agree, but if new cars are made affordable to the public, more cars will sell, and the amount perhaps compensated. The country would economize on foreign currency because the old cars need millions of dollars of spare parts, much higher fuel consumption and a predicted pollution level that will force the country to import millions of gas masks soon. The simple solution of reducing the customs duty on new vehicles during meetings had a violent response from the podium. In reality, though the maximum level of import duty in Ethiopia should not exceed the level of 10% if the government considers the welfare of its population.

There are many similar observations, but I do not intend to bore the reader with them.

The EPRDF started to issue identity cards, upon which there was a place dedicated to ethnicity; a dangerous and divisive question. This was an upsetting turn of events with the ability to divide Ethiopia into groups. No sense and no meaning, how can this build unity among people? Divisions in religious beliefs for example, even among believers in Christ, there are dozens of sects and divisions, with differing ways of worship. Ethnicity also for me is the same; humanity started with one group and separated later. The question on the identity cards was a problem for Armenians because the government naturally did not have Armenians on the list of ethnic groups. As it was requirement you would not get an ID Card. The clerk filling the form insisted on having the information. When I saidI was Armenian; she told me it could not be, it is not on my list, upon my insistence she asked me which Ethiopian language I speak, when I said, Amharic, she noted down Amhara. During the renewal, they agreed to put Armenian as ethnicity. I jokingly told them, now I need a seat in the parliament, at which point they panicked and wanted to change it and started quoting the directive that that twenty thousand people living in an area speaking a different language can claim ethnicity. We need to look into unification and not division. I am Armenian and Ethiopian, and I proudly call myself EthioArmenian.

The first exit visa I applied for after the Derg regime also met with controversy. My rejected application went to the head of the department who asked me why I am considered an Ethiopian. I told him the same way he was. He did not like my reply, the same way I did not appreciate his question. He was angry, so I showed him the proof of my Ethiopian Nationality from the time of the Emperor, he was skeptical. So, I told him, "unlike you, I do not have another passport in my pocket." The shock in his eyes confirmed my accusation at which point I gave him a brief history of the things that Armenians did for Ethiopia, and he finally agreed to sign my exit visa.

The Immigration Office finally waived the requirement of an exit visa and started renewing the passports for five years instead of two years. The Nationality question persists. Recently a youngster came to me asking if I can talk to the Embassy of the Federation of Russia so that they issue him a passport. His question shocked me. His grandfather is half Armenian, and he is dark in color but because his family name is Keorhadjian, an Armenian name, they told him to go to the Embassy of Armenia, and when he explained that the Armenian Embassy is in Cairo they referred him to the Russian Embassy.

The youngster was named after the great grandfather Abraham Keorhadjian, who suffered the ordeals of a concentration camp in exile in Italy during the Italian occupation of Ethiopia. Abraham Keorhadjian was the overseer of the palace and refused to give the Italians the keys to the treasury, so he with his whole family experienced life in a concentration camp, when exiled to Italy. Two of his children suffered irreversible mental trauma from the awful experience. I wrote a brief note addressed to the Immigration giving a historical explanation about the Keorhadjian family and the ethnic mix of Abraham, whose "Armenian" ancestry is below five percent.

The election of 2005 showed the degree of the unpopularity of the government. The real results that appeared at the first instance disappeared immediately and the canvas ballot boxes were transported and refilled with the desired votes for the ruling party. And for days there was paper burning which went out of control and the fire brigade intervened. This is no speculation, this is a witness account.

The ruling party on Wednesday before the Sunday polls opened, organized a rally for the support of the ruling party, and they announced a huge number, it was the biggest rally witnessed in Addis Ababa to date, and in the television announcement they named the rally "A Storm." But the next day an unprepared, unorchestrated people's rally dwarfed the organized one by at least tenfold, the ruling party felt the imminent defeat. The independent papers called it "The Tsunami." On Friday, I saw four or five SUVs with no plates and completely tinted glasses enter the palace. As with the London conference, there was no need for the vote of the people of Ethiopia.

Late at night, the engines of a heavy Hercules airplane thundered over Addis Ababa. The climate of world politics of the day took the decision and gave the green light to the ruling party, to rig the votes.

CHAPTER SIXTEEN

It is from the eyes of my entrepreneurial adventures that I recall so much of what it was like to live through the experiences of every possible difficulty; investing during times of extreme shortages, extreme and corrupt bureaucracy, constant changes of officials and even the danger of wrongful imprisonment or death. The anticipation of better times for the economic growth of the country and the fact that the government admitted being mistaken in certain aspects towards the end of the Derg era, gave us hope to venture into something new in our life.

Once the court acquitted Salpi, we traveled to Nairobi, where I attended the biannual Rubber Conference organized by Polysar, Columbian Carbon Black, Kordsa, and Monsanto. Salpi made the tour of the Safari parks of Kenya and during that trip made the life-changing decision to resign from Hagbes and become self-employed.

We decided to invest in Ethiopia convinced that our experience was good for Ethiopia. What we didn't take into account was the policies of the EPRDF, that reserved all opportunities for growth for the privileged few and not for people like us. We had not expected to have an authoritarian replace a similar communist regime. EPRDF micromanaged the private sector and scrutinized the activities of small exporters like us, which the Prime Minister proudly demonstrated during meetings.

My 25 years of experience acquired by supplying industrial chemicals to almost all the industries in Ethiopia, provided me with vast and comprehensive information on the requirements of each sector and an ability to identify items that could be import-substitute or else are exportable.

I was approached by many for ideas and, based on my advice, many individuals launched successful manufacturing enterprises, like shoes, contact adhesives, wood adhesives, paint, plastic moldings, soap, abattoirs, and even tanneries. In the family, we discussed the various opportunities and decided on producing pre-molded shoe counters, something new for Ethiopia, an item substituting an import.

President Mengistu chose American army boots that have a leather-board counter as stiffener at the back part, and over its last few years, the Derg had decided to improve the clothing and the military boots for the soldiers. Too little, too late. The Ethiopian army had over a million soldiers and a militia. Tikur Abbay Shoe Factory's capacity was more than 3000 pairs per day. We calculated a project to supply this requirement initially. I provided the ready-made counters to Tikur Abbay, so I knew the disadvantages of importing the ready-made stiffeners. The plan was feasible, and we got the necessary permits and investment licenses.

We got the land and applied for a construction permit, and we got it, but there was no construction material available. The country did not have cement, hollow-block, wood, iron, roofing material, nor anything else for construction. Even quarried stone was in short supply. Based on the investment licenses we got priority but the queue for cement was over four months long, and for roofing material six months. Wood was nonexistent. Despite this, we launched the project. Our attachment to Ethiopia was unbreakable, so profound that we optimistically continued with our investment. Who would invest in such an atmosphere? Only blind optimists or delusional persons.

The shoe-counters required the import of leather-board. To avoid an import, we performed a second feasibility study to produce vegetable-tanned leather as a replacement to imported leather-board. We had some trials done in Europe developing a recipe for the leather to be successfully used instead of leather-board. The application of the second license was successful. The Derg believed in a one person one license policy, so my wife Mary filled in the necessary forms. Governments put restricting laws to show power, pretending to protect the interest of the whole population, without realizing that limiting investors limits the resources of the government. At a later date, we imported the leather-board machine, which we eventually sold as scrap metal.

I could fill volumes retelling the nightmares that kept us awake at night and the hoops we had to jump through to purchase all the building materials, but I will omit it, except for this one account that describes our determination for the project. It was when we had to purchase the cement.

After a four-month queue, it was finally our assigned date to get the cement. We tentatively secured a truck to load the material and went to the distribution center. Our name was not on the list amongst the lucky winner. We asked, and we were told to check the next day. After a week of next day checks our name was not on the list. Finally, Salpi went there and tried to contact the "Lord" of cement. He managed to avoid Salpi for two hours. Desperate to get things going, Salpi took the chin of someone double her size in her hand and asked, "when will our name be on the list"? He could not avoid the pressure. His effort to postpone it for tomorrow did not work with Salpi and he was extremely offended that a small woman grabbed his chin in front of a big audience. This led him to put our name on the list. It was not a favor, it was our right and it was our principle not to bribe persons, to whom the government gave a position where he had the power to better himself. He is not to blame. In any country, a government needs to study the influence the position creates when there is no competition.

While cement under Haile Selassie's reign was Birr 4.08/100 Kg and readily available, under the Derg's rule, laws were issued, and the "EPRDF" followed with directives that created private monopolies, or cartels and just a few people controlled the price. The cement price and distribution in Ethiopia has a problem still to this day. Even after many big cement factories like Deriba and Dangote started production, neither sold the cement matching international rates up to now. The corrupted system of distribution prevails to protect a factory which is removed from the true market. The "Lord of Cement" is perhaps replaced by a "Queen of Cement."

Unfortunately that evening an earlier announcement delivered news that ordered all trucks had to go to the war front. The next morning we collected the delivery order to get our cement from Mugher Cement Factory some 50 kilometers from Addis Ababa to the west. We knew that area as children because the Sandfords had a farm where our father tuned their piano twice a year and where we picked strawberries. After the nationalization of the land, strawberries along with other vegetables that Mulofarm produced went extinct in Ethiopia, and the farm was buried under the dust of the cement factory. We got the delivery order but there was no truck. We tried every possibility; private exporters, friends, and relatives but without success. We understood they had good reason since the government forced the transport vehicles on the road redirected towards a losing war. Finally, we contacted an unknown person Salpi met in a government office, who gave his telephone number, in case we needed assistance in resolving problems created by the laws and thousands of directives issued by the government and governmental offices and authorities. He responded to our call, and we met in a café. Naïvely, we gave him the receipt together with the delivery order, and he left with the fate of our 40 tons of cement in the hands of this unknown person.

He didn't even have an office, and we didn't even know his address. Three excruciatingly long days passed with no sign of him and no answers to our calls. On the next day which was a Saturday, we went to the factory, and the little hope that we built on our way there, dimmed when there was no sight of any truck on the road. In the afternoon, while inspecting the clearing of the access road to the factory, there was the sound of an overloaded engine going uphill. From far we could see an orange truck, all orange trucks with that particular hue belonged to the Ethiopian Road Authority. The orange lorry passed us taking all our hope with it because we knew for sure that a government truck does not serve the public. To our surprise it went into our compound, we followed with anticipation thinking of a logical reason that a government vehicle would enter our compound. Then we saw the triumphant gentleman who greeted us; he had all the right to be proud of his achievement; he achieved the impossible. He saw the relief on our face and said – here is the cement, you trusted me, and I did what I had to do. He could have easily sold the truckload on the black market in a matter of a few minutes, but our trust made him act honorably.

Despite the financial difficulties and the shortages in the country, we met honorable people who delivered our building materials. The honesty was encouraging giving hope for a bright future.

We installed the shoe counter machines, and before the room was ready with the lighting, we got the order from Tikur Abbay Shoe Factory for the counters of the military boots. It was a promising start, and we worked day and night to deliver the first order at the same time training employees. The first order of a hundred thousand pairs out of the million pairs expected was out when the government change occurred and the military was dismissed. The EPRDF soldiers did not wear boots, their footwear was a sandal made from scrap tire and they said they won the war because the Derg soldier lacked mobility due to the weight of their boots. A few years later they wore the same military boots, but because of the different distribution system and many reduced quantities, Tikur Abbay Shoe Factory abandoned the production of the sophisticated shoe and replaced it with a simpler model. Our enterprise was destined to fall into oblivion and the machinery under a sheet of canvas for protection from the dust.

My first experience with the tanning industry was with Ethiopian Tannery. In their first tender, we participated with two British Companies and one Austrian Company, Ellis Jones, Hodgson Tanning Company and Reichold Chemie for the finishing items. Ethiopian Tannery awarded us several products, and we provided them with technical services. During the trials, I noticed the diversity and the challenge of the leather industry which attracted me.

Despite that, we had the license, but we lacked the resources for starting in the tanning industry.

Mary's uncle, Artin Avakian had a tannery near the Armenian Cemetery, on land leased from the heirs of Hagop Baghdassarian, who owned a vast area. One Sunday I asked her if she remembers the place, which she did so I asked her to show me the factory. I gave my card and told the guard to give it to the owner and ask him to contact me. A few days later Bedada Chale called me. I understood he wanted to start production of pickled sheepskin for export, he had done some trials, but there was not much evidence. I organized the production for him and we met in Paris in the "Semaine du Cuir" exhibition, where I helped him also by introducing him to machinery manufacturers and even potential buyers of pickled sheepskin. He acknowledged my contribution to his start many times. After a trip to our head office in London, he visited me and advised me to start my own business. I did not know what prompted him to do so, but he promised to help me. When I told him, I intended to begin leather production he enthusiastically approved and assured me of his assistance. My ambition blinded me and following the failure of the first project due to factors beyond our control, we forged ahead with the idea of a tannery.

During a trip to Kenya, I met a Sudanese Armenian with significant experience in starting tanneries, especially in Africa. He gave me a lot of advice and parted exchanging telephone numbers. During my next visit, he invited me to the tannery they were starting, providing me with plenty of new ideas and solutions for an economical start-up of our production. From the discussions, I learned that there was a demand for East African wet-blue hides. As not many tanneries exported the semi-tanned hides from Ethiopia, I decided to concentrate on the output of cowhides. Another aspect I noticed was the number of contraband hides from Ethiopia unloaded in Kenya. Our savings secured the purchase of the wood for the tanning drums and the fleshing machines from Germany. All the parameters were there for the success of the intended investment, except the finance for a starting up. The first machinery and the drums arrived a few days before the change of government.

I received a call one day from Varouj, the gentleman I met in Nairobi. He asked me to meet him in the first-class lounge of Ethiopian Airlines where he would be for the next two hours. I immediately arranged a permit and visited him there. He had an offer for me. He wanted to invest in the project. I was forthcoming and explained the difficulties and the restrictions involved and the risks in Ethiopia, but he assured me that none of that affected his proposal. Joyful, hopeful and deep in thought, I returned to my office. His offer was too good to be true. It meant the realization of a dream that I had never imagined could really happen.

A few months later Varouj visited us in Ethiopia; his offer was still valid. He wanted to check the availability in Addis of pumps, hardware and other equipment besides the visit to the factory. The remarks during his stay regarding future co-operation were both encouraging and plausible. His nephew accompanied him on the next visit. The conversation covered practical aspects of co-operation and the suggestion of working as threesome emerged. The British company was to cover marketing and quality control. It was suggested to include a raw trader to guarantee the supply of hides and skins and us running the Ethiopian operation. After two months with a verbal agreement between Varouj, Bedada and us, things were in action. A surprise followed. The British Company shipped machinery, equipment, and chemicals without the prior permits, putting everything in the fast track, causing a lot of pressure. We managed the import and cleared the items. Bedada, as agreed, provided the used gears and gearboxes, and the installation was on its way. However, before the final agreement, Bedada pulled out demanding a considerable sum, which we agreed upon even though it put a dent in the working capital. The initial draft agreement seemed workable, but when it came to the signing of the final articles of association, there were some points, which clashed with the laws of Ethiopia and we declined signing it. The partnership broke. We ended up in debt to both partners.

Startups under these conditions were tenuous, to say the least.

With great difficulty, we overcame them and started the export of wet-blue hides. Different from the traditional way, we introduced the production of full cowhides without cutting them to sides, and we packed the product on pallets instead of the conventional jute bags. We built a loading dock where the trucks approached, and we loaded twelve pallets into a twenty-foot container, ready for shipment. The other innovation that we did in hide production was the salting of the fresh hides we collected in Bishoftu; our hopes paid off as many raw traders followed our examples and salted the hides instead of the traditional pegging and air-drying. The quality of our product was superior to the others for which we received a premium price. The price we got created some envy amongst the other tanneries, who had never achieved the value we got per square foot of the hides. In a crucial meeting, a few voiced their opinion in the Leather Association regarding the extra ten cents suppliers voluntarily paid us.

We were the targets of systematic harassment before we even started the production of leather. With government change, the administrator of the region changed. Unlike his predecessor, the new one was a bigot and suffered from an inferiority complex, fitting the parameters that Meles Zenawi revealed when he was confronted by journalists regarding the appointment of some officials. Meles Zenawi said, "I may appoint anyone, even ignorant persons, as long as they are loyal to the party and its principals." The regional administrator exercised his immense power over an area bigger than dukedoms in Europe. Whenever he felt, he sent his henchmen on motorbike and ordered us to close the factory. Their main reason provided was polluting the environment. There was no production. Incidentally, the only tannery with a functioning effluent treatment plant was ours and many experts even from UNIDO copied our technology and my questions served a few persons to become famous in treatment plants.

One day the closure order was severe. We dismissed the construction workers and the next day received a call from the Ministry of Health in Addis Ababa. The officer, holding a report in his hand, informed us of a complaint about radiation pollution from our factory. I thought someone was quoting from the film Erin Brockovich which was available at shops for rental at the time. He claimed the report was from a very highly placed official and asked to visit the premises with radiation experts to verify. After his visit, he cleared us to continue our work. A top EPRDF personnel with his cronies enjoyed the beautiful villa of uncle Elias next to our factory during the weekends. The buddies of this senior government official had other aspirations for the land allocated to us, which belonged to our parents before nationalization.

There was also another neighbor a radical extremist professor, who sought power with EPRDF and volunteered to protect the environment of Bishoftu. He pushed many ideas to eliminate the properties overlooking the lake, in which case his property could become the one on the forefront. The administrator presented us with a long list of names who claimed our production was hazardous to their health. One absurd accusation was the miscarriage of the eight-month pregnant woman living seven kilometers away from our factory. There was the horsecart driver's allegation that his horse lost its hair when he washed it from the water flowing out of our compound. After a full week's investigation to find the water, they couldn't spot a single drop of water coming out of our compound. Our learned neighbor put in a false report about us discharging effluent to the lake following the discoloration of the lake. He initiated the clearance of the crater of the lake for people to stroll around the lake and the eroded soil from the wide pathway was the culprit for the discoloration, but he tried to blame us. No water left our compound except the water we supplied to the neighborhood. Before starting production, we had the lake water analyzed by a certified government institution, and once we started production, we closely followed the parameters as our recipes depended mostly on the quality of the raw water temperature, alkalinity, hardness, and other specifications.

In October 2004 the Prime Minister of the United Kingdom, the Honorable Sir Tony Blair, visited Ethiopia. Instigated by the Ministry of Industry, the leather association prepared an exhibition at the newly inaugurated United Nations Economic Commission for Africa compound, and all the newcomers in the industry who were leading the association did the preparatory work. At the last minute, an emergency general assembly was undemocratically called brought by the old guard by appointment to lead the association. This created the downward slope of the association or as one member put it the "travel agency." The old guard and the educated president used the association for their benefit only.

The exhibition was a success, but unfortunately, it further strengthened the government's desire to micromanage the industry, creating an opening for high ranking government officials to become involved in the leather sector. The appointed committee of the association, concerned with personal gain, unconsciously dug the grave of the leather industry of Ethiopia when in 2008 the government levied an export tax on semi-processed leather.

The Armenians innovated the traditional preservation of leather into an industry in Ethiopia at the end of the 19th century. Yessayi Garigian with knowledge of hides from Ethiopia, established a tannery at the outskirts of Harar, near a small creek where he also built his residence and a beautiful garden, as mentioned in the book "Oasis" by Roupen Vorperian. Roupen Vorperian was a correspondent of the "Daily Mail" stationed in Djibouti. In August and September when temperatures in Djibouti reached 50 degrees Celcius, Vorperian spent time with his family at the property of Yessayi Garigian. Garigian had a few Armenian tanners working for him, like Artin Kalaydjian and later Stepan Darakdjian, the father of Mardiros Darakdjian, the entrepreneur who created the "Darmar" Tannery and Shoe Factory.

Darmar was by far the biggest industry in Ethiopia following HVA the Dutch-owned Sugar company until the emergence of Addis Tyre S.C. and Ethiopian Rubber and Canvas Shoe Factory. Another Armenian visionary Alex Karibian conceived the vision, but unfortunately, he was robbed of his dreams when Ethiopia and Czechoslovakia realized the projects as an intergovernmental co-operation.

The other giant in the leather sector a big industry in Ethiopia was ASSCO which stands for Avedis Sevadjian and Sons Company. Assco also owned a tannery and a shoe factory, while Darmar concentrated on civilian shoes. Assco specialized in military boots. The research work in animal breeding for the betterment of the meat and hides, the experiments on the production of natural rubber and production of wattle extract for tanning by Aassco are worthy of mention as historical contributions of Armenians in Ethiopia.

Darmar produced over a thousand pairs of shoes per day and exported some to Europe and the Middle East. Assco also produced around a thousand pairs of the military footwear of different types. Before the nationalization, they each employed 350 employees in the shoe production and after the confiscation of the industries, the numbers reversed, a thousand workers, produced 350 pairs per day.

The skin of Ethiopian "hair-sheep" famous for its fine grain, thinness and with a high tensile strength had a market in the gloving industry. For decades companies like Pittards purchased these initially in the raw and eventually as pickled material. Pickling means removing the hair and acidifying the skin for temporary preservation until further processing to convert it to leather. The first tanneries exporting pickled skins were, Darmar, Ethiopian Pickling from Addis Ababa, and Assuad Tannery from Asmara. The premium price paid to the exporters of pickled skin resulted in killing the initiative to produce fully tanned gloving leather, which of course required many years of experience and expertise. Naturally, government-owned factories lacked ambition and were challenged.

The big numbers from export income created an influx of many who, with a mere investment of two drums and a fleshing machine, gave rise to unhealthy competition and shortage of supply. The result? The hoarding of the raw material, which also caused a deterioration in quality. While traditionally the yield was about 50% (the highest grade) and 5 to 10% (the lowest grade), after the mushrooming of several tanneries, the process yielded only 17%

of the highest quality. More than 20% was rejected and the rest was mediocre. Due to the lower grading, Ethiopia could no longer meet the requirements of the world market. The glovers looked for other suppliers, creating competition, and adding to the lower aggregate price from the production. Ethiopian tanners faced competition in the world market succumbing to a lower export price. Picklers had to borrow to sustain their business.

The other product well known for its high quality was the Bati goatskin. The natural tight structure of the flesh side of the pelt is ideal for the production of suede leather. Unfortunately, the fashion world dictates the requirement of suede, and its demand varies year-to-year according to the fashion demand, therefore it is highly seasonal. Suede jackets are not always trendy, and when not in need, the market of wet blue goatskin diminishes, often lasting for a few years. But when in demand, all qualities sell at a reasonably high price. The mushroomed tanneries jumped into this as well and as explained above led to a deterioration in quality with similar consequences.

The Ethiopian cowhide is of inferior quality. The highest grade is equivalent to the rejects of European hides. It is small, has no substance, with very loose grain, and because of the Zebu hump, it is divided into two sides, fetching a meager price in the world market. On top of these factors, the cattle in Ethiopia moves freely all over the country and have a lot of surface damage from thorns, not to mention the traditional curing of diseases, branding, and treatment of the animal during herding and finally the flay cuts on the skin due to the conventional slaughter methods. The business of wet-blue hides is highly dependent on the world economy. When the world economy is at its peak, the high-quality big cowhides are used to produce upholstery material for cars, furniture, and airplanes. When the world economy goes into depression, textile and artificial material overtake the upholstery market. This creates a a surplus of high-quality raw material from the U.S.A., Europe, and South America, available for shoe wear and accessories causing the demand for cow leather of poor quality to decrease, which affects the export of Ethiopia.

Our plan to produce wet-blue cowhides followed my visit to a tannery in New York state, in the Northern United States, where our pickled sheepskin was up against a much superior quality from Ethiopia. I wanted to see the condition of our packing. There I saw the blue drums with the pickled sheepskin from the competition. While we tried to secure raw material for this order, we came across these drums in a store belonging to a wheeler-dealer in Bishoftu. Sensing the illicit nature of this, we thanked the person and tried to forget about it. He made an attractive offer but venturing into it would guarantee good profit while securing our startup capital, but due to its illegal nature, we declined the offer. Purchasing that stock was like winning the jackpot of a lottery ticket, but we distanced ourselves from all temptations and by all means, avoided linking to it. Someone else did and in meetings boasted that his knowledge on raw selection secured him over 80% of the highest grade. If I ignore what I witnessed in Gloversville, the only conclusion to draw from that comment of the elderly gentlemen is that he had a special "capability" to see the quality of the skin through the cover of the dense hair.

We felt that creating a dialogue forum for all the tanneries was necessary, so we organized a dinner invitation at the Armenian club to discuss strategies for competing against other upcoming tanneries in Africa and Yemen who were targeting the same customers buying from Ethiopia. The danger alarm was on. The report I presented graphically showing the correlation of all the parameters on the cost of production taking into consideration the selection yield, the raw material price, the chemical input, and the overhead costs and showing that the amount paid by tanneries at that time for the raw material was over the aggregate sales price. The comments rumored around my presentation concluded that the dinner was a gimmick by me to sell chemicals. One tanner told me that I had not considered "the cream" in my calculations. The cream meaning the premium price Pittards paid for the highest grades. I distanced myself from making further comments. My predictions proved to be correct and everyone experienced losses and borrowed heavily from the banks to recover. They also failed to understand the reason for the downward trend in the industry.

All tanneries in the race were unfit for it because they proceeded with passion, jealousy, and unhealthy rivalry when what they needed to do was to cooperate. The future of the Ethiopian Leather Industry was not the concern of any of them as long as they proved their strength and many bragged childishly about their manhood. The biggest supplier of fresh hides is the Addis Ababa Abattoirs, and the tanneries had a cartel system that took turns collecting the slaughtered. We asked to take turns, but we were rejected. On the next tender, we offered the highest workable price, that the abattoir had no records of in its entire existence. We took delivery of the cowhides up to the next bid. The cartel invited us to take turns; we accepted. A few years later two other tanneries joined the system even though one was 800 kilometers away from Addis Ababa and the non-refrigerated journey under the scorching sun was not good for the hides. Looking at the immediate acceptance of the two made me think about our initial rejection. Was this bigotry or ignorance? I still don't know for sure.

After Tony Blair's visit, the government took the initiative to convince Pittards to prepare two privately owned tanneries for the production of gloving leather. As usual, the reward went to the same beneficiaries, who always secured grants and loans of machinery and technical support from UNIDO. The whole system was one-sided. The association, the ministry, and the leather institute stood for the same few tanneries. Visitors to Ethiopia who asked for suppliers of wet-blue cow leather never got our name from the association despite the fact that the secretary owed his prominent promotion to Salpi. Keeping us off the list was the gratitude we received. Without any assistance and support, we made it, even provoking the envy of the privileged. The government based the initiative on a supposition that all picklers deliver their product to the four who would finish the leather. But they failed to consider the piling up of the lower grades with the suppliers, who will drown under the debt of the accumulated rejects. Each tanner borrowed again to try finishing leather. Pittards took over Ethiopian Tannery and the plan failed.

The Privatization Agency called for bids to privatize the nationalized or rather illegally appropriated tanneries. One of the first was Modjo Tannery, located ideally with a vast area with a high production capacity of skins, and the possibility of expansion, alongside a river. The sales concluded, and Bedada declared the winner. A few months later Addis Tannery was on the list and our customers East Hides from London showed interest in investing in a tannery in Ethiopia in partnership with us. Addis Tannery is the oldest one in Addis Ababa built on a creek, in a deep gorge with no possibility of growth and with arrears to settle. The bid opened. The highest bid lacked the necessary documents required by the bid document, and we were the second. Our offer was higher than the sales price of Modjo Tannery, but the committee decided to re-tender. The reasons being obvious, we did not participate in the repeated bid. Later a friend said that we did not know how to proceed. Yes, that is true because we would not have a government official as a silent partner with us and bigotry against us was a factor.

The Ministry of Industry had a ridiculous system of celebrating those who exported the most with winning a cup at an annual meeting of all exporters. The immature behavior from most who received it was so obvious that it created an unhealthy rivalry, price hikes and working at a loss which kept resulting in further deterioration of the industry. The ailing industry under the unhealthy competition was weakening, while the traders of hides and skins, taking advantage of the situation created an artificial shortage so that at a later date as vultures they attacked the corpse for the last piece of meat.

Without proper study and with the usual miscalculation of the consequences, the Ministry pushed forward the idea of discouraging semi-processed leather by levying export duty and trusted the task of deciding the percentages to the "Association." During the meeting, everyone whose interests were in skins decided to tax goatskin at 5, sheepskin at 10 and for cowhides, they earmarked 20 percent, despite the poor quality of hides for the export market. One of the most persuasive arguments in the meeting to levy a higher percentage on the export of the wet-blue-hides was to target our tannery. The reason was the extra benefit we secured with our quality, the convincing phrase was "they have benefitted a lot" — the discussion of the meeting leaked by shocked board members later. It took them a few years to tell me this to my face and confirm it and I cannot say it shocked me. I reached a point where nothing in these proceedings shocked me anymore.

The government announced the law, which largely targeted our business and hit the final nail on the coffin of the industry. And when mocked in the Shanghai exhibition by Ethiopia's traditional buyers, the minister had the tax levy raised to over 100 percent, banning even the crust export allowed in the beginning. Emotional and divisive decisions ruined the industry. No tannery in Ethiopia had the technology, the machinery, the know-how, the trained human resources and the market for what the government was aiming. Simultaneously they were freezing bank loans to tanneries and when challenged to reconsider the decision, they sarcastically said that the EPRDF has no reverse gear, that immature statement became their motto in order not to revise the wrong decision. But it is true, because of the lack of wisdom to back it up they drove the industry over a cliff. Even ten years and hundreds of millions of dollars investment, Ethiopia is not ready to export finished leather in any significant quantity. What is worse, I know of at least one tannery which continued to sell abroad semi-processed leather illegally, but without any severe or real sanctions applied, when customs officers seized the containers.

Under the first law, we honored our contracts sustaining heavy losses. Commodity trade has negligible margins and paying 20% on the export drained our capital. We approached the bank to restructure our loan, and the best answer was "It is a directive" from the National Bank we cannot do it. We very well knew what the reply would be from the "cemetery of development of Ethiopia" National Bank, but we tried to appeal to them anyways. The secretary of a deputy murmured in reply to our plea "there was yet another directive." The thousands of "directives" that govern Ethiopia are

"I Want to Die with a Flag"

the tools of ignorance, laziness, indifference which pave the way to corruption. For the resurrection of development in Ethiopia instead of burning the "chibo" during the next celebration of the "Finding of the True Cross" all the directives issued for the past 25 years should replace the bonfire. While we were being refused an affiliated party tannery received loans and support. We sent an appeal letter to Prime Minister Meles Zenawi. Surely it never reached him and was pushed under a pile of applications. We also asked Hailemariam Dessalegne to intervene, making sure that he got our request. He did, but the banks played one against the other like a ping-pong ball mockingly sending us to and fro. The unwritten secret directive blocked even the plea of the Prime Minister at the time. The same system that grants loans based on telephonic instructions without collateral in billions refused to restructure our insignificant debt. Our request was legitimate; we failed in our payments because the government issued a law. The law needed to include the restructuring of the loan guaranteed by the government for a certain number of years.

The negative incentive for pushing the leather sector to added value was a delusion on the part of the government, the leather institute, and the association. The objective was to go into finished goods, and without proper research, the ministry encouraged the production of the shoe with a few European companies. These depleted the stock of sheepskin, using the delicate hair sheep, suitable for gloving, for shoe wear production. The export price of the shoe was below the value of the skin. The tragic truth was a pair of shoes, with a sheep leather upper fetched US$ 8.00 per pair for Ethiopia, while being sold at Euro 150.00/pair in Europe. Despite that advantage, the shoe projects also failed further destroying the hope of sheepskin gloving export of Ethiopia. The tanneries in desperation continued selling below cost, to keep the factories open.

An aspect never talked about is the fact that with more processing, many more job opportunities would open, but that also didn't happen. Only two of our ex-employees currently work in a tannery, all the rest are jobless or work on construction sites. Many tanneries under pressure reduced production, and many workers lost their jobs. We employed about 120 permanent and temporary employees, with a payroll of over a hundred thousand Birr a month, generating taxes for the government. We paid taxes in the hundreds of thousands. Now we employ about thirty of the senior staff and pay no taxes as the company operates at a loss and the payroll is below thirty thousand. And most of the tanneries owned by Ethiopians are in a similar situation. Whoever claims to be making a profit is living in a dream world.

Compared to other tanneries our debt to the bank was minimal. With the infamous law, we lost our customers. At the same time we received a letter to relocate our factory as the zoning of Bishoftu changed. Without the restructuring of the loan, there was no way to proceed. We saw this coming a few years earlier, so we researched possibilities. We approached the Modjo municipality, who rejected our request saying there was no more space for another tannery. Meanwhile, later four new ones mushroomed in the area with much bigger land than our requirement. We moved towards another direction. We pinpointed a spot outside Sululta and pushed forward in the relocation of our tannery. In the end, the environment office of the municipality said the possible pollution of the water-table would affect the future water supply projects for Addis Ababa and refused the allocation. But a few months later a Chinese company built a tannery on the same plot, with no effluent treatment plant. We tried the Butajira road, but the "King" of the region, did not even look at our application, with a rejection we abandoned the idea of pursuing the relocation idea. The government suggested, and the administrations rejected, and no one supported it. All our efforts were met with unfair blocking after blocking after blocking, but we were persistent.

Despite being the first tanners in Ethiopia to export finished crocodile leather and goatskin fur leather to fashion houses in Europe, long before the law, we never contemplated producing crust or finished leather. All calculations showed that without the support of the government and the banks no factory could upgrade its tannery to manufacture leather. As for the production of accessories, it turned out that buying the finished product from other tanneries was cheaper than producing it, So we jumped on this idea and started the production of leather jackets, purses, wallets, industrial gloves, and handbags. We built a clientele in this field during the past ten years, but due to lack of working capital, it is still in its infancy. There exists a Development Bank of Ethiopia, but it serves the foreign investors, some of whom fled leaving the bank with canvas tents as collateral. But for Ethiopians, who did not have connections with Government officials, under directives, the bank refused loans. Talking to a foreign investor, he expressed with admiration about the efficiency of the bank. It took us three years to get a rejection letter from that admirable institution so forgive me if I am less than impressed with their highly regarded efficiency.

While the Commercial Bank denied loans and restructuring to tanneries, we read in the newspapers that, they gave hundreds of millions to big companies especially multinational foreign investors, whose turnover is bigger than the budget of Ethiopia a few times over. Who can comprehend such anomaly?

Our various efforts to talk to the Minister and the State Minister had no solution. On multiple occasions, they discarded our request for restructuring our loan and more than once we received sarcastic comments that to assist certain companies is useless; they were referring to us. Even the head of the Leather Institute made this unwelcomed comment. The problem was the limited capacity of their understanding; they were slow with no vision for the future at all. Only eight years later the government started to push the banks to restructure the loans and those of the favored ones. When the government issued a law to drive the industry into added value, they didn't consider that the tanneries needed more financing. Without the financing to import over eighteen different types of machinery, various instruments for quality tests and forty-three additional chemicals to start production the tanneries would not be able to produce at the level they wanted. It required at least five years before they could build an export market. The government was forcing a toddler into the marathon race.

The many obstacles created for us, made us stop the production of leather altogether. Our decision to distance ourselves from leather production was a wise one. The insurmountable obstacles were many, persecution, unequal treatment, a chronic foreign exchange shortage, the abominable supply of electricity and the involvement of foreign companies with disproportionate privileges in the sector. This was the cherry on top of the cake - the government convened the parliament to pass decrees allowing foreigners to operate in businesses restricted for foreigners.

A branch of the African Union from Zambia commissioned us to produce giveaways for a meeting in Addis Ababa. For the delivery of 3000 bags, we faced a problem with the power. The electricity was out for two consecutive days and hundreds of times intermittently. We complained to the electricity company whose response was, "work with a generator." There was also a shortage of fuel at that time. Without fuel the generator does not generate electricity, and at that period Ethiopia sold power to the neighboring countries. No doubt the payment is in foreign exchange, but at the expense of additional import of fuel and failing the industry. We managed to deliver the bags, calling back the employees from their homes, when the power was on at odd hours to meet a deadline.

Just when we started regular production of accessories, the bank decided to recall the loan. They targeted us ignoring the other tanneries because they had sufficient collateral against the debt. They acted unfairly, and I dare say even illegally when we challenged their action. Another directive, which by the way we were never able to see, allowed them to go ahead with their decision. Before auctioning the assets of the company with limited liabilities, they tendered our private property. Of course, the neighbor of the office had provided them with an incentive to put the house on the market, which was so apparent on the day when we delivered the keys to the neighbor. The bank officials foreseeing the handing over were elated and could not sustain their smile and were unnecessarily familiar and friendly with the buyer calling the buyer "Habibi" even – his name may have been Habib – but Habibi in Arabic is an endearment, and the lady seemed to be saying it as an endearment with a big smile. Unfortunately for the neighbor and luckily for us, there was another bidder in the auction, and the price soared up beyond any expectation. We paid our debt but ended up without the property in an area which developed to become the heart of the banking and insurance headquarters of Ethiopia. Were we the subject of persecution or discrimination? The answer for me is, **both**.

Apart from leather, all other industries faced similar problems due to the immaturity or perhaps the self-interest of the leadership in the Ministry of Industry.

CHAPTER SEVENTEEN

Ethiopia is a place that can enchant you with its natural beauty, history and its humanity. There is a gorgeous landscape of mountains, water and wildlife and a lively kaleidoscope of cultural, ethnic and language diversity. Ethiopia is my homeland. It's where I was born, where I grew older and where experiences and situation I went through perhaps made me wiser. Everything that I am is a result of all the experiences Ethiopia has given me. Is it any wonder that it's the country I love? Far from ideal or calm at least now there is a semblance of peace and the economy is growing at a "speedy and steady pace" according to government statistics. Over my lifetime, I've confronted many systems, companies, and people trying to make it hard for me to succeed in business and I've seen the kind of senseless horrors no one should ever have to see. Through many periods of political instability - living through three regime changes - I married my wife Mary, and we raised our family in Ethiopia and still, without hesitation I can say that even with all the problems and there are plenty of problems I am completely devoted to my country.

In 2010 EPRDF won a "huge majority" 99% in parliamentary elections and Meles Zenawi became Prime Minister for a fourth term. Hailemariam Dessalegne was the vice premier under Prime Minister Melles Zenawi; I wonder… if Meles would have known of his untimely demise could anyone have predicted that someone from the Southern Peoples Democratic Party would dream of becoming the Prime Minister? Well, that's what happened. When Zenawi died in 2012, Vice Prime Minister Hailemariam Desalegn took over, and in 2015 May EPRDF scored another victory by gaining 100% of the votes.

The governing principle of EPRDF was to divide the country ethnically based on linguistic differences. Following the philosophy of "divide and rule," this one party ruled Ethiopia creating enmity between the divisions. Inter-party relations meant that one faction had more influence in it than others, but this is still very much shrouded in layers of complicated structures I am only just beginning to understand. In any case, that EPRDF is a multiparty coalition is a tenuous pretense whereby a small group of people appointed a few officials that belonged to different parties within, but the prime positions somehow always managed to go to a small group of inner inner circle members. Another strange appointment saw the Amhara leader Demeke Mekonen as the vice to Hailemariam Dessalegne. TPLF was probably too busy to notice such trivial details like who occupied the position of vice premier.

Starting in 2016, there was an outbreak of anti-government protests, and the Government declared a state of emergency. The copycat parliament of the TPLF passed emergency laws a few times in 2016 and 2017. These enforcements against unarmed rioters was a profound cause for instability within its ranks, but the one in 2018 was decisive.

Hailemariam Dessalegne refused to sign it and instead decided to resign and finally cut the TPLF strings controlling him. As I always suspected and mentioned to friends, Hailemariam had a few trump cards up his sleeve, which was a very well-kept secret without the slightest indication even from the grapevine of Addis Ababa. The discipline and coordination of the rioters, who had Addis Ababa surrounded, suggested the existence of a central high-ranking leadership. My speculations about this proved right. This went on for many months.

Our ancestors likely had no understanding about ethnic divisions in Ethiopia. They would have been shocked to know the number of ethnicities there are now. It's said that 80 different ethnic groups call Ethiopia home today and there were not that many ethnic divisions a century ago in Ethiopia. As far as I know, the past Armenians knew few clans within Ethiopia because ethnicity was generally not an issue. External provocation usually propagates racial differences, and these varieties that mushroomed after EPRDF took power were not of consequence before the 20th century. During that period not many foreigners, missionaries, politicians, narrow-minded ethnic nationalists, opportunists, and divisive historians, could visit rural Ethiopia, to pinpoint differences that lead to racial or clannish dissections. Except for the small secluded communities, our ancestors differentiated three main ethnic divisions from the south of Ethiopia, amongst those who sought work in Addis Ababa. They distinguished the Gurage, Wolayita, and Hadiya. At the time, they only knew the names that are today considered derogatory. Upon the election and confirmation of Hailemariam Dessalegne as Prime Minister, I remembered the expression from our elders who used to say - be careful of the "Hadiya" they dig from underneath. The coup was from within.

Ethiopians who sought solutions from God hoped for change to come following the appointment and election of Hailemariam Dessalegne as Prime Minister. In his first days as Prime Minister, he moved around freely; he attended the annual Beaujolais party in the Sheraton Addis on the first Thursday of December, unannounced, unguarded. The management and security of the hotel panicked, but he liked to move around independently with friends instead of bodyguards meeting the people. Despite my quiet demeanor during such parties, I came face-to-face with our new Prime Minister and congratulated him. But that was the last time we saw him mingling with people freely. During the rest of his premiership, for entirely other reasons, he remained heavily guarded like his predecessor Meles Zenawi inaccessible in the ivory tower surrounded by the TPLF.

Hailemariam lost his composure, and as time passed the people noticed frustration both in his voice and choice of words. He started using the language of his predecessors, something strange for him, and for me, under the evident pressure. It wasn't a surprise when his resignation came. It was a matter of time, and from the looks of it, he was part of a plan to bring about a significant change.

The whole coup in the parliament resembled a well-choreographed show. Hailemariam resigned, Demeke offered his position to Lemma Megerssa but Lemma (not a member of the parliament) passed Demeke's offer to Dr. Abiy, and Dr. Abiy Ahmed got the premiership. Brilliant coordination and execution of a plan. The group of four, with Abiy Ahmed's leadership, launched a comprehensive program of political reform that was unexpected and welcomed with a peaceful solution to what was building up into a genocidal civil war. The group of four deserve the honor of being placed amongst the heroes of Ethiopia for staving off a genocide or a massive civil war at the minimum. It is early yet to judge their full achievements and possible failures, but this in itself is a commendable first step.

When popular unrest persists, governments succumb. There are many examples like the success of Hitler in Germany, the peaceful struggle instigated by Mahatma Gandhi in India, the triumph of Nelson Mandela from his prison cell, the Arab uprising in Egypt and Tunisia. The "velvet" revolution led by Nicole Pashinyan in Armenia last year and - as I call it - the "silken" revolution led by Abiy Ahmed and his group in Ethiopia can pave the path towards a bright and peaceful future. The way of Nelson Mandela hopefully prevails in Ethiopia.

Mengistu Hailemariam compared himself with Emperor Theodoros. If we accept Mengistu as the equivalent of Emperor Theodoros, then Meles Zenawi pairs with Emperor Yohannes IV and that makes Abiy Ahmed the counterpart to Emperor Menelik II.

Both Menelik and Abbiy have the dream of a united Ethiopia. The eras and the methods applied are different, but the principle of a united Ethiopia that both Menelik and Abiy follow is the same. In the present, a multicultural multi-ethnic country can be the only solution, and Abiy rightly in his speeches uses the term "Meddemer" or "addition" not unification. Unfortunately, the term "unification" in Ethiopia has a somehow violent undertone. However, I believe federalism for Ethiopia is a controversial and expensive proposition, the demarcation of boundaries of the jurisdiction of each state is difficult to define and needs a full set of government officials for each federal state. The prediction of unforeseen problems of the future is impossible as it is not clear yet how many regions may wish to form a separate state.

With the principles of "addition" of Dr. Abiy, the party name "EPRDF" Ethiopian Peoples loses whatever it stood for. A revolution is an uprising of the people against a government; Democracy means the rule of the people and so far, we have not seen a glimpse of democracy. The word "Front" adopted from the days of armed struggle represents a group against the government. How can one govern a country and still call itself "revolutionary" and "front?" Does the title have a meaning, or it is just a mockery? The name EPRDF (Ethiopian Peoples Revolutionary Democratic Front) contains controversial words that clash with reality and with each other. The only indisputable word is Ethiopia, which seems it is there for convenience, to confuse people. Nothing the EPRDF did, has anything to do with the concept of a united Ethiopia.

The reforms that Dr. Abiy plans on were unthinkable even just a short while back. The restructuring work awaiting Dr. Abiy is not only to clean up the corrupted administration, but also to include the EPRDF party itself, starting with the name. There are many like me whose vote will go to Dr. Abiy, but with a party name like EPRDF with a manifesto that is revolutionary, many will restrain themselves from voting for that party which has a history that is contrary to the principles announced by Dr. Abiy. As for "The Federal Democratic Republic of Ethiopia" with no comments I suffice saying it is too long. "Ethiopia" is a more meaningful alternative to the long phrase.

Will Abiy be able to sustain his popularity? The people of Ethiopia did accept the change with hope and rejoiced; however, they are not easily manipulated. The Ethiopian population is politically savvy, and over the past four decades they're trained to analyze situations, Ethiopians are highly political in their thinking. Rhetoric is not enough: Politicians who make promises will have to do what they say and say what they do. People expect delivery. During my student days in the Soviet Union, while I was in a taxi with an older gentleman for a driver, Brezhnev was delivering a speech. I asked my driver what Brezhnev was saying. He told me it was all just rhetoric pretending a growth. Although I spoke the Eastern Armenian dialect fluently, he knew I was a diaspora Armenian and said, my son, everything in the Soviet is a pretense, the government pretends that they are paying us and we pretend that we are working for them. Years later I saw this phrase in Times or Newsweek. He was teaching me about the gap between the people and the government. A leader should avoid creating that pretense, people have immense patience and can wait, but it does not mean they accept readily. Leaders must prove they're worthy of being trusted. Mengistu executed the sixty officials, Meles reproached the symbol of Ethiopia saying it's nothing but a piece of cloth, a distorted phrase alienating him. Abiy is a brilliant orator and a capable negotiator, but concentrating only on the politics and forthcoming elections, with no economic benefits to the people, he could slip away from their support and adoration.

There are too many leaders in high positions who don't stand by what they profess. Too many leaders who don't seem to really care about the nation; the people. They exert control, demean, threaten, spend money in the wrong places widening the gap between "them" and "us." The emperors did it considering that it was their birthright to rule, but "elected" leaders really must refrain from it. There is no foundation for the pedestals on which they stand unless the people put it there for them to stand on. Unfortunately, what we have seen up to now, is grabbing the "throne" and regarding the population as unimportant and below the governing elite. That tendency is dangerous; it breeds overconfidence, which leads to mistakes that cause unpopularity and the eventual failure of government. A governing body has nothing to govern over without its people. It's crucial for leaders to be aware of the danger, to keep away from demeaning the people, both morally and materially. The fuel shortages, electricity cuts and soaring prices demoralize the people, and the achieved successes can quickly deteriorate. Things that may seem unimportant unimportant to leaders are vital to the people. With fuel shortages and interrupted supply of electric power at increased prices, cooking food becomes strenuous and the euphoria quickly vanishes. Any action should consider the needs of the country first, before that of a neighbor.

Oratory skills and spontaneity are qualities that leaders need to have, but excessive use can give way to a slip of the tongue as we've seen happen with preceding leaders who come up with phrases like "which people?" or "a flag is a piece of cloth" as uttered by Ato Meles. And "I poked the butts of the generals with the bayonet" as announced proudly by Mengistu. Every country has its examples that haunt the thoughts of their people, and they do not pardon, but elaborate on the mistakes and create jokes about it. This is not okay anywhere, at any time.

At the end of my fourth year in university in Soviet Armenia, my professor of "Scientific Communism" said that he planned to include questions from Leonid Brezhnev's speech. We were advised to follow it attentively. This convention was some time at the end of May 1973 and the examinations were in July. I listened for about three days, but by day four and five I could hardly pay attention any more as the same question kept occupying my thoughts, "who is he trying to convince"? During this era, between Mao, Castro, and Brezhnev, I don't know who wins the prize on lengthy addresses to the nation. Mengistu also tried to join the club, but he was too far behind his mentors as he was at heart a military man and even he was bored with meaningless blather. When I summarized Brezhnev's speech for the exam, all I could come up with was less than a page. Lengthy statements seem an attempt to persuade not only the party members but also themselves, as the people are too far ahead from them, the leaders need to reach them. It is impossible to deny the power of an orator who can stir the passion and extreme nationalism in people, which as history shows us can lead to dangerous consequences, like what happened in Germany before the Second World War.

The present administration, for whom peace is its primary objective, will benefit the country if peace remains the primary concern on the agenda, a path towards truth and reconciliation can follow. When punishment is the primary agenda, it takes precedence and stalls progress towards peace, growth, and stability. There are many crimes committed against the county and the Ethiopian people and undoubtedly many wishes to see the perpetrators punished, but if punishing them becomes the principle, then the primary objective will vanish.

Regarding the forthcoming elections in May 2020, many think it is too early, but it is the prescribed date from the last "elections." If postponed it will cause antagonism, and if held, people will complain that it's unfair. The opposition parties need to act quickly and build the trust and confidence of the people. Judging by some of the speeches of opposition leaders, it is evident that the opposition has been absent from the country for many years and has lost touch with the reality of the Ethiopia of today. They have no time to lose; they need to start to understand the mentality and campaigning beginning from the grassroots.

It is time to end the false reports from the ministries, the fake numbers from the central statistics, the immensely powerful positions in the government hierarchy, the poor administration of government offices, the unavailability and unanswerability of the civil servant. It is time to limit the meetings in the government offices so real, sustainable change can finally take place. The people do not buy the lies, so why should the government lie?

Over the past forty-four years, Ethiopia suffered in so many ways. God answered the prayers of all Ethiopians giving a chance to eradicate everything that immature governance created such as the unwelcomed rivalry, displacement, clashes, ethnic chaos, and poverty. One regime overthrew another brutal government. The famine in Wello that triggered the revolt against the Haile Selassie regime reached unprecedented levels during those decades. Let all mythical boundaries between leadership and people break, and we will finally experience a real government of the people and for the people.

It is not my intention to drift into the analysis of the future of Ethiopia. I want Ethiopia to be great for everyone living in the country including the insignificant number of EthioArmenians.

EPILOGUE

The observations and conversations within the pages of this book reflect my concerns, convictions and deep-rooted love for a country that I call home.

It's true. I have very strong beliefs about the welfare of my beloved country, and I share all my inner thoughts with the public so the struggles and survivals of Ethiopia can be seen and felt through my eyes. The eyes of a man who was there through this part of our history.

I have the profound hope that by sharing the experiences of my family with Ethiopia it will open the hearts and minds of those in a position to help bring reform. Every step we take towards that end can help someone to correct a wrong path or a controversial law.

When I pre-warned about the imminent dangers the tanning industry faced sixteen years ago, it was with the hope of fixing a weak trend, but instead, it was met with skepticism and sarcasm. The probability that the content of my memories will displease some people is likely. That's not my goal. Truth and transparency are not criticism, they are the precursors to improvement, for the sake of all.

I aim to reach the Ethiopian masses, and if any of my experiences help even only one Ethiopian out of the 100 million, then I will consider this a success. And, if it gives insight to lawmakers to acknowledge weakened or problem areas, well, that would mean immense jubilation for me.

Many friends ask me if my memoirs are in Armenian to which I say, "I have to share my experiences with my compatriots, the Ethiopians and so I am writing in English as my Amharic is not of the literary level."

This is not a book of the History of the Armenians in Ethiopia. I have a duty to fulfill to influence my motherland so for now – until l write that book – this is the book I am compelled to bring into the country - one Armenian in his homeland Ethiopia who saw what he saw and tells it through the eyes and emotions of his experience. Now is a time of great hope and promise for Ethiopia and this is my way of contributing to the growing optimism that is alive in this generation of all my fellow countrymen.

And, I have my final message to the leadership of Ethiopia. It is my wish to see them endowed with the wisdom of great leaders, like the self-sacrificing Mahatma Gandhi and the broad-minded Nelson Mandella.

May the almighty as always protect Ethiopia.

My great great uncle Roupen Vorperian wrote an ode dedicated to Emperor Menelik II in 1905. In 1913 after the death of Menelik he added two verses wishing the Great Emperor, the King of the EthioArmenians a peaceful eternal life. I translated the one written in 1905 and rewrote it in Amharic and in English inspired by the original piece of Armenian poetry:

ՄԵՆԵԼԻՔ

Խաւարակուռ Ափրիկէի կուրծքին վրան,
Ուր հորիզոնը կ՚երկարի դէպ ովկիան,
Ըմբոստ լեռներն ուր ամայքէն կը թռչին
                         Ամբաւութեան,
Հնչեց մէկ օր ծայնն «Առիւծին Յուդայի»
Որոտումի նման գոռաց մէկ վայրկեան
Սարսուռն մ՚առին անապատներն ամայի
                         Եւ անսահման:
Փայլակնացայտ նայուածքն իրեն Արամազդ,
Կայծակին շողքն առաւ իրեն զերդ մական,
Ու ծնրադրեց իրեն մեն մէկ Աստուծոյ,
                         Ազատութեան:
Ցեղերու մութ անկերպարան քաոսէն,
Ծնունդ տուաւ իր մեծագոր կայսրութեան,
Ու խորտակեց Աստուայի մէջ մոլորուն
                         Սէք Եւրոպան,
Չինկալ երբեք։ Մնաց միշտ վես ու հսկայ,
Մէկ օր միայն իր հուռ աչքերն մռայլեցան,
Ու լացաւ ան բաղդին վրայ հետագայ
                         Հէք Հայութեան:
Ճակատն օծուած Հայուն անմահ միւռոնով,
Գիրկը բացաւ տարահալած մեր ցեղին,
Եւ զգացինք մեզ անձանօթ իր գորով,
                         Գութի ոգին:

ምኒሊክ

በጨለመው የአፍሪቃ ምድር
ባህር ከሚጥሱ ድንበሮቹ
ሰማይን ከሚነኩ ተራሮቹ
ከባህር የሚዝቁ ሽለቆቹ
ነጎድጓድ ጩከቱን አንድ ቀን፤
አሰማ የዩዳው አንበሳ፤
በረሃዉን ሁሉ አንቀጥቅቶ
ድምበር እና ባህርን አሻግሮ።
ብሩህ አይኖቹ እንደ መብረቅ
ከዘራውም የአለመቀህ
ነበልባል፤ ቢሆንም ተምበርክኮ
ከፈጣሪው ነጻነትን ለመነ።
የዝርያ ሁክት ያጨለመውን
ታላቁ ኢትዮጵያን ገነባ መልሶ
በአድዋም የአውሮፓውያን
እብሪተኛውን ጦር ደምሶ
አሸነፈም፤ ተሳነ ክብርና ኃይል፤
አንዴ ግን አይኖቹ ለብሶ እምባ
አለቀሰ፤ ለሩቁ የአርመን ህዝብ
በደረሰው አሰቃቂ ጭፍጨፋ
በጥንታዊ የአርመን ሜሮን፤ ግንባሩ
የተቀባው ይህ ጀግና፤ ጉያውን
ክፍቶ ተቀበለ የኛን ህዝብ
የማያውቁት ርህራሄን ለግሶ

ከአርመንኛ የተተረጎመ
(ጥቅምት 2011)

Menelik

Inspired by

Roupen Vorpeian, 1905

Amid darkened Africa,
Horizons reaching oceans
And mountains touching the skies
Depressions beneath the seas,

A voice from, thundered one day
Roared the Lion of Judah
Sending quivers through deserts
Across borders beyond seas.

His gaze shone, like lightning
His staff like Zeus, Thunderbolt,
He aimed to might and glory
But knelt and prayed to be free.

From dark ethnic chaos,
Forged a mighty great empire,
And in Aduwa, he shattered
The fledgling ambition of Rome.

Never failed, was always wise,
Once, shadows covered his eyes
He cried for the tragic doom
Of faraway Armenia.

His forehead anointed with
Ageless Armenian myrtle
He embraced our nation
Bestowed on them compassion.

(October 2018)

HOPE

Amid a reborn Africa,
Horizons short to oceans,
And mountains up the skies,
Depressions lower than seas,

A voice from gentle, one day
Pleaded for calm and unity,
Sending a message through deserts,
Across borders to the neighbors.

Reaching to all clear and loud
For real peace and amnesty,
Opened borders put down arms,
Offering peace and friendship.

Through the dark ethnic chaos,
They shone a light of new hope,
With their wisdom, they shattered
The imminent civil war.

May God give them further wisdom,
And long life to see it through
The rebirth of the united,
The great nation, Ethiopia.

Ode to
Abiye Ahmed
Lemma Megerssa
Demeke Mekonen
Hailemariam Dessalegne
(October 2018)

KEVORK NALBANDIAN

Kevork Nalbandian was born in Aintab (modern name Gaziantep) in Turkey. He was the second of the Nerses Nalbandian children, six brothers, and one sister, (Haroutioun, Kevork, Setrag, Missak, Garabed and Hagop and sister Nourizza). All the six played the violin.

Kevork Nalbandian had a factory employing women weaving textile by hand. In 1915 he and the family fled to Aleppo, where his older brother was working as an interpreter for the British contingent stationed in Syria. In Aleppo, he tried several businesses including a transport business in partnership with Haroutioun and Missak. They had two trucks transporting goods from Aleppo to Tehran. Missak was stationed in Tehran, and finally, the company broke up, and Missak remained in Tehran.

In 1924 as a political activist in the Social Democratic Party (Hinchagyan) he had to flee from Aleppo and arrived in Jerusalem.

In 1923 Itegue Menen (wife of Haile Selassie) traveled to Jerusalem and visited the Armenian Sourp Hagop (Saint James) monastery and was impressed with the monastery that had many orphans in its care. Among the ~~many~~ children were the "40 orphans," who were saved by a priest Father Hovhannes Simeonian in the western Armenian region of Van and Moush, He had brought them via Iraq to Jerusalem between 1918 and 1920. The following year in 1924, Ras Teferi (at the time the regent of Ethiopia who later became Emperor Haile Selassie of Ethiopia) on his way to Geneva to present the country to the League of Nations, visited Jerusalem. At the Saint Hagop Armenian Monastery of Jerusalem where the brass band of the "40 orphans," received him. Subsequently, he agreed with the Armenian Patriarch of Jerusalem Yeghishe Tourian to engage the orphans as Ethiopia's brass band guaranteeing education for them. The "40 orphans" were between 12 and 18 years of age. The following picture is of the 40 orphans with Patriarch Yeghishe Tourian and the envoy of Ras Teferi.

Ն. Վ.Ս. Թէքլէի օսեփեան հրամանաւրէր՝ երէաաղեի Ս. Յակոբայ վանքի
Մայբի գրան առք՝ Ա.Ա.Ա. Ս. եղիել Ս. Գառաբապի հետ.

By a twist of faith, the music teacher of the "40 orphans" declined to go to Ethiopia, and after some negotiations, between the Armenian General Benevolent Union (AGBU) and the Ethiopian Government, Kevork Nalbandian replaced him and joined the group in Port Said. Together with Father Hovhannes Simeonian, he accompanied the "40 orphans" to Ethiopia, arriving in Addis Ababa on the 6th of September 1924. As was a tradition the group met the Armenian community near the large shola tree on the Belay Zeleke road. They initially resided at a house belonging to Lidj Iyassu (The grandson of Emperor Menelik II). The following picture is Kevork Nalbandian training the 40 orphans.

Apart from his duty as the musical director of the palace, Keork Nalbandian was the music teacher at the Teferi Mekonen School. Although some unsuccessful attempts were made to play Ethiopian music with European instruments, it was Kevork Nalbandian who successfully trained Ethiopian youngsters to play the instruments. (The following picture is Teferi Mekonen school with Kevork Nalbandian and three other Armenian teachers Sarkis Aintablian, Stepan Papazian, and Vahram Mistik.)

He composed anthems for Ras Teferi, Empress Zewditu, Crown Prince Assfa Wossen and later the National Anthem of Ethiopia, which was the official anthem until 1974.

The following is a letter from the government addressed to Kevork Nalbandian dated 14 October 1928, to train the youngsters to play the National Anthem on Haile Selassie's coronation. In 2013 there was a debate in the Addis Ababa trying to prove that the National Anthem "Ethiopia Hoy" composed by Kevork Nalbandian was composed at a much date, based on a few words in the anthem that suggest that it dates to Haile Selassie's triumphant return from exile. This letter disproves all arguments and shatters all doubts on the dispute forever.

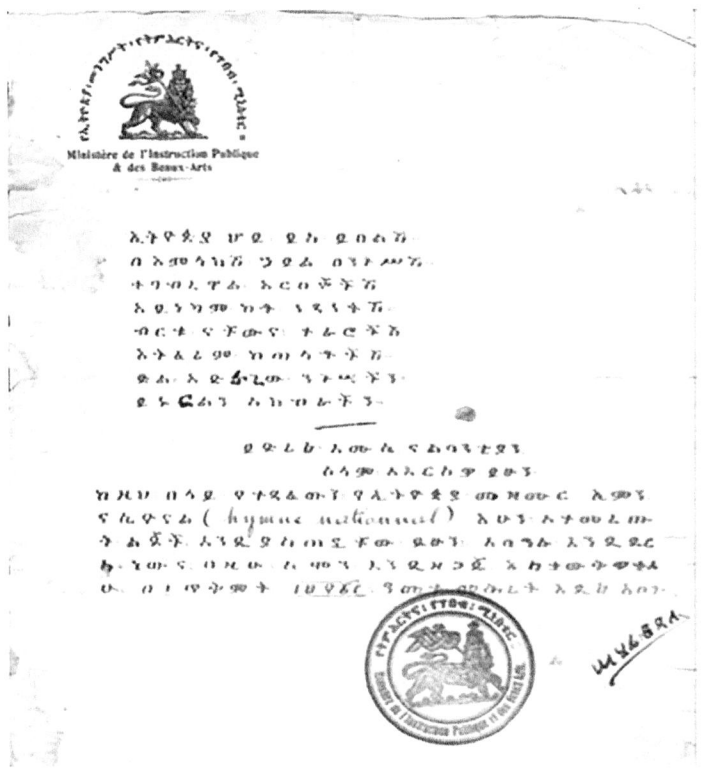

Kevork Nalbandian has also written four musicals but unfortunately, we only have evidence about one of them, which is a satirical drama named the Adventures of Gebre-Mariam of Gondar. In 1934 it was performed, upon the request of the audience the performance was repeated several times with great success.

With the Italian occupation, Kevork Nalbandian was initially put under house arrest because he worked in the palace and had a military rank of Captain in the Imperial Bodyguard, he was later set free. In 1932 his brother Haroutioun and then Setrag joined him in Ethiopia. The family of Haroutioun came to Ethiopia in 1938. His brothers Hagop a music teacher in the Ethiopian Police Force followed them later.

Kevork Nalbandian organized the Armenian Church choir for the occasion of the placing of the foundation of the church. Later the church choir was re-organized by Kevork's nephew Nerses, the son of Haroutioun. (The following is a picture of Kevork Nalbandian as a deacon on the day of the laying of the foundation stone of the Saint George Armenian Church.

Following the footsteps of his uncle, Nerses Nalbandian trained, composed and arranged Ethiopian folklore and popular music for modern instruments.

According to the correspondence with the Armenian General Benevolent Union, who organized his trip to Ethiopia, Kevork Nalbandian and his wife Elise had two children, one of whom died very young. Jirayr grew up in Ethiopia, and attended "Collegio Armeno Mourad Raphael," in Venice for his education. After finishing his studies, he could not return to Ethiopia because of the Second World War, during which he joined the resistance movement. Later he came to Ethiopia and worked in the bank now known as the Commercial Bank of Ethiopia.

The arrival of Kevork Nalbandian and the "40 orphans" (known as "Arba Lidjoch" in Amharic), helped Ethiopia build an image as a country with humanitarian and modernization values.

NERSES NALBANDIAN

Nerses Nalbandian was born on the 15th of March in 1915. His exact registered birthplace of Nerses is Aintab (Gaziantep), although this is unclear as the family escaped the atrocities committed against the Armenian population in Eastern Turkey during that period and the Haroutioun Nalbandian family which originated in Aintab, between 1915 and 1921, had been in Killis, Hama and eventually settled in Aleppo.

Nerses Nalbandian attended Cilician National School in Aleppo for his primary education and continued his secondary education in Aleppo College. He studied violin for one year with his uncle Hagop Nalbandian and took piano lessons from Azniv Manougian. In 1932 his father Haroutioun lost his job as an interpreter and was forced to join his brother Kevork in Ethiopia with the hope of bringing the family to Addis Ababa. While Haroutioun was establishing himself, Italy conquered Ethiopia, and the communication with the family became difficult. Finally, with the efforts of Kevork Nalbandian, the family got a special permit from the Italian administration in Ethiopia. Nartouhi Nalbandian with her children Nerses, Marie, Hrant, and Puzant arrived Addis Ababa on the 15th of November 1938.

During the six years of separation from his father in Aleppo, Nerses was obliged to interrupt his education and start teaching, music, violin, and piano and organizing a choir to support the family. In 1934 Nerses was appointed as choirmaster in the Armenian Church of Iskenderun. His sister Marie joined him as a teacher in the National School of Iskenderun. After spending two years in Iskenderun, they returned to Aleppo, where they continued teaching and looking after the family. While in Iskenderun Nerses started studying the Armenian Ecclesiastical music and based on the interpretation of Armenian Notations of Nigoghos Tashdjian, he transcribed all the hymnal and the breviary to European notations. This life-long project has produced a unique manuscript of over 1200 pages.

Nerses Nalbandian in Aleppo.

While in Aleppo, he organized a chamber orchestra performing classical pieces and Armenian music arranged for the band by himself. Subsequently, he became the church choirmaster in Aleppo.

The love of music pushed Nerses to continue studying it by extensive reading; correspondence and following the trends of the times thus acquiring knowledge on symphonic music, brass band music, jazz music, and contemporary music.

The first thing Nerses did upon arrival in Addis Ababa was to form the Mouradian Choir, and on the 24th of January 1939, he became the choir-master of the Saint Kevork Armenian church of Addis Ababa. In addition to teaching in the Armenian School popular music and ecclesiastic chants, many youngsters started taking piano and violin lessons privately from him, and he trained a few of them to play on the church organ to accompany the Mouradian choir for the holy mass.

The students of Nerses Nalbandian in Taytu Hotel hall after a concert about 1952.

The group who performed Sos-Vartiter 1946.

The Mouradian choir achieved great success not only in the church but with regular concerts and performances. Nerses successfully organized a complete musical performance of Armenian operettas like "Sos and Vartiter" and Arshin Mal-alan." The soprano soloist in the act of Vartiter is Elise Vorperian, the future wife of Nerses. Haroutioun Guevherian, the tenor soloist on her left and Hrant Nalbandian, the bass soloist on the right.

The Armenian Community of Ethiopia was able to keep the Armenian Culture alive thanks to the relentless efforts of Nerses Nalbandian. After the concert of the Glee Club Choir in the University hall, the Director of the Haile Selassie I University Lucien Mati has written. "The performance of your choir has been of the highest level, whereby the performance discipline and precision were evident" He has also added saying that "the audience was captivated particularly with the performance of "Africa Africa" and the "National Anthem of Ethiopia" by the choir.

Mouradian Choir 1966 on the steps of Ararat Club.

Nerses Nalbandian taught, directed and composed Armenian music. He also arranged music for choir and orchestra for special occasions. He sometimes even arranged classical pieces to be played with two pianos, for example, the Saber Dance of Aram Khachaturian.

Nerses Nalbandian also performed with the Musical Society of Ethiopia performing pieces from Gilbert and Sulivan. He also was the lead violinist in the group that performed chamber music. His brothers Hrant and Puzant were involved in these performances.

"I Want to Die with a Flag"

The musical society the YMCA around 1962–1968.

During the weekends he organized a band playing dance music at the Taytu Hotel, where the expatriate community enjoyed their time of leisure. They had a vast repertoire of contemporary popular music, which he transcribed listening to the radio and imported the music sheets arranging them for the instruments of the orchestra.

Nerses with the accordion, his brothers Hrant and Puzant with the violin Hagop Meneshian on the double bass, Torkom Aslanian on the drums 1954 –1957

Nerses Nalbandian was also very involved in teaching music to youths. He taught at the Armenian Kevorkoff school music, solfeggio, choir and religious music, (the mass to the girls and the deacon parts to the boys) many of the school students, served the church in Ethiopia and outside Ethiopia thanks to the knowledge they had grasped under his guidance and tutorship. Apart from the Armenian school he also taught at the Nazareth school.

Nerses Nalbandian with the Nazareth School choir welcoming His Imperial Majesty Haile Selassie I.

At the University Hall conducting the Glee Club Choir 1962-1963.

He also organized a choir in the Haile Selassie I University, strengthening the female voices using the Nazareth school girls at the Glee Club. The choir performed for the first time Ethiopian popular music in four voices by a choir accompanied by an orchestra. The Glee Club concerts became very popular until the banning of all social activities in the University under the pretext that students with reactionary political affiliation used it as their forum.

Nerses was a very disciplined and hard worker. Apart from the above mentioned he also taught at the Theological College upon the invitation of Bishop Terenig Poladian, who was the first Dean of the Theological College organized in a modern way. After the departure of Bishop Poladian Nerses Nalbandian received a letter where the new dean of the theological college canceled the music lessons because of poor attendance.

At the Theological College with the teaching staff Bishop Terenig Poladian in the middle.

He was among the founders of the of Music School together with Skinner and Topalian and worked there as a violin and choir teacher. This school later became the Yared Music School.

Nersses Nalbandian also taught music and choir at the School of Commerce and the school of the blind. Together with Miss Skinner, Mrs. Azad Topalian, he was instrumental in organizing a music school initially in the compound of the Nazareth School, (before the transfer of Nazareth from Ager Fiqir Theatre locality to its present place). The music school went to a house in Sidist Kilo near Medhane Alem Church and later to a villa opposite the current Yared Music School and finally to the University compound before the construction of the Yared Music School by the Bulgarian government.

The Music School staff in the University Compound Sidist Kilo Campus 1965.

Conducting the Yared Music School choir 1972.

Besides the teaching at various schools, Nerses Nalbandian was the musical director of Haile Selassie Theatre (Presently called National Theatre). He was appointed to that position initially at the Municipality of Addis Ababa in 1951 where together with his students in the Municipality they became the orchestra of the Haile Selassie I Theatre in 1958. It is here that he composed and arranged all the music based on the lyrics and melodies by Merawi Setot, Kassa Wolde, Teferra Abunewold, Getachew Debalke, Tesfaye Sahlu, Getu Ayele, Menelik Wssenachew, Melkamu Tebedje, Tesfaye Lemma, Getachew Mekuria, Tesfaye Abebe, Getachew Abdi, Getachew Tilahun, Getachew Ayele, Girma Negash and the like. He also brought many singers to stardom like Telala Kebede, Fikirte Dessalegne. He used to record the melody, and the lyric transcribed it to musical notation and arranged it for the orchestra and taught the singer the song. Usually, he did it overnight ready for the next day.

For a brief period, he left the theatre and worked for the Police Orchestra for whom he created an anthem. He upgraded the police orchestra such that, through his creations and arrangements Alemayehu Eshete, Wegayehu Deginetu, and Hirut Bekele achieved stardom in Ethiopia. While working for the police, he also trained the Police Military Band.

Nerses was commissioned by the government to compose music for special occasions. On the opening of the formation of the African Unity, he was asked to write an anthem for the Organization of African Unity. He produced "Africa Africa" which was first performed by the Mouradian Choir. The government wanted him to train a choir for the first performance of "Africa Africa" in the Haile Selassie I Theatre. He trained a group and until the last day he conducted it. Due to the controversies created he led the choir and the band from behind the curtain, while a pseudo-conductor moved his arms visible to the audience. He also wrote a welcome song in honor of Jomo Kenyata on his first visit to Ethiopia after the independence of Kenya.

Nerses Nalbandian with the National Theatre Orchestra.

Nerses Nalbandian with the National Theatre Orchestra.

Nerses continued working after the overthrow of the Haile Selassie regime. Initially, the intention was to replace him, but when the attempts of organizing a choir with the volunteer students failed in every way, the Government appointed him as the conductor of the 250 student's choir.

The success of the choir while ultimately pleasing, also meant a lot of work for Nerses as the Government used to make last-minute decisions to perform in the theatre or the Meskel Square or the stadium.

In appreciation of the extra work, the Ethiopian Government included him on the team for the Festac in Nigeria (The African Music Festival). For the preparation of the exotic music Nerses Nalbandian worked with traditional musical instruments of the Asosa region, which had become a hit in Nigeria.

All their instruments were tuned ay Nerses Nalbandian.

Nerses Nalbandian conducting the 250 students' choir in the National Theatre.

In 1975, Nerses Nalbandian was asked by Maître Laureate Tsegaye Gebremedhin to participate in the competition for the National Anthem of Ethiopia for the Dergue Regime. The National Theatre also wished to present an anthem as a group with Nerses's composition. His pieces won, and Atnafu Abate summoned him to the palace, to inform him. There he was told to get ready to go to Moscow for the recordings. However, a few days later he was told that his music is too advanced for a developing country and that he should help to select an anthem composed by other musicians.

Nerses in the National Theatre with the 250 strong Idget be Hibret choir in 1976.

Nerses Nalbandian also composed the score of the first Ethiopian film "Hirut Abbatwa Mann New." He also composed the music for many musicals like "Theodoros," "Atsme Beyegetsu," "Ha Hu Besidiist War," "Enat Ager Tenu" and others.

Nerses was one of the first to understand the Ethiopian musical modes Ambasel, Bati, Emahoy, and Tizeta which were the basic modes played on the Ethiopian pentatonic musical instruments and all his arrangements are typically Ethiopian because he had kept all his compositions and orchestration within the framework of the modalities of Ethiopian traditional music.

Nerses's musical efforts, achievements and the legacy it created resonates throughout modern Ethiopian music to this day.

Aside from being a musician, choirmaster, composer, conductor, and teacher, Nerses was also an expert piano tuner and repaired pianos including the furniture. He also repaired violins and violin bows. He generously and often shared his vast knowledge in any of these areas with others. He spoke Armenian, Amharic, English, French, Italian, Turkish, Arabic, and German. His relaxation pastime was doing the crossword puzzle in Italian.

BIOGRAPHY

Vartkes Nalbandian is a 3rd Generation Ethiopian-Armenian born in Addis Ababa. Growing up in Ethiopia in the 1960s and growing older and wiser since then, Vartkes followed his primary education in the Armenian Kevorkoff School in Ethiopia, his secondary school in Melkonian Educational Institute in Nicosia in Cyprus and ultimately his Masters in Electro-Mechanical Engineering from Soviet Armenia from the Yerevan Polytechnic Institute.

Vartkes is a dedicated family man and counts among his pillars of strength the five family members who are central to his story. These include his lovely, loving and wonderful wife of four decades, Mary and their intelligent and accomplished children namely Garen (son), Elise(daughter) and Raffi(son) as well as his sister Salpi, a singular individual with an-she of the indomitable sister.

Vartkes is a devout churchgoer (or in his case Archdeacon who leads a mass regularly). He would not argue too much if you used the word "community elder" but is not sure about the word "elder" as he does not feel that old. With the life, he has led and his accomplishments, he still feels fighting fit and is more than willing to share his memories of the three of four regime changes in Ethiopia with an incisive analysis of the undercurrents of the country.

He has worked in business for many years in many sectors, industries and sales of products he has a wealth of experience in how to live and work in Ethiopia which he will admit is not easy.

Vartkes is the custodian of EthioArmenian history, and as such he is regularly called on to contribute to the rich tapestry of Addis Ababa's history which is very much part of the Ethio-Armenian story.

In this, the debut novel he shares his experiences of growing up and growing older in Ethiopia as Ethiopia transformed and grew. His memories of long times past show the idyllic give way to challenges and the issue of identity, country and work in Ethiopia mirrors and mimics the lives of all Ethiopians but with an additional twist.

Vartkes lives in Addis Ababa with his family.

Printed in Great Britain
by Amazon